Philosophy & Human Nature

Readings assembled by
Laird Addis
University of Iowa

The McGraw-Hill Companies, Inc.
Primis Custom Publishing

New York St. Louis San Francisco Auckland Bogotá
Caracas Lisbon London Madrid Mexico Milan Montreal
New Delhi Paris San Juan Singapore Sydney Tokyo Toronto

McGraw·Hill
A Division of The McGraw·Hill Companies

Philosophy & Human Nature

Copyright © 1999, 1998 by The McGraw-Hill Companies, Inc. All rights reserved. Printed in the United States of America. Except as permitted under the United States Copyright Act of 1976, no part of this publication may be reproduced or distributed in any form or by any means, or stored in a data base retrieval system, without prior written permission of the publisher.

McGraw-Hill's Primis Custom Series consists of products that are produced from camera-ready copy. Peer review, class testing, and accuracy are primarily the responsibility of the author(s).

1 2 3 4 5 6 7 8 9 0 QSR QSR 9 0 9

ISBN 0-07-235250-7

Editor: Judy Wetherington
Cover Designer: Pat Koch
Printer/Binder: Quebecor Printing Dubuque, Inc.

Table of Contents

The Origin and Development of Psychoanalysis   **Sigmund Freud**
    1

    Introduction (by Eliseo Vivas)
    First Lecture   17
    Second Lecture   25
    Third Lecture   30
    Fourth Lecture   39
    Fifth Lecture   45

Mysticism and Logic   **Bertrand Russell**

    Mysticism and Logic   51
    The Place of Science in a Liberal Education   71
    On Scientific Method in Philosophy   79

Language and Mind (selected chapters)   **Noam Chomsky**

    Linguistic Contributions to the Study of Mind: Past   97
    Linguistic Contributions to the Study of Mind: Present (excerpts)   117
    Linguistic Contributions to the Study of Mind: Future   123
    Form and Meaning in Natural Languages   137

Acknowledgments

Pages 1 – 50   Public Domain, 1910

Pages 51 – 70   This essay appeared in the *Hibbert Journal* on July, 1914. Public Domain.

Pages 71 – 78   This essay appeared in two of *The New Statesman*, May 24, and May 31, 1913. Public Domain.

Pages 79 – 96   'On Scientific Method in Philosophy' was a Herbert Spencer lecture at Oxford in 1914.

Pages 97-150   From *Language and Mind*, enlarged edition by Noam Chomsky. Copyright © 1968 by Harcourt Brace Jovanovich, Inc. Used with permission

INTRODUCTION

These five lectures, delivered by Freud to an audience gathered at Clark University in 1910, are an excellent introduction to Freudian psychology. Written down after their delivery in his invariably terse, lucid style, they present no obstacle to the reader wishing to obtain an elementary grasp of Freud's basic ideas about the way the mind works and mental illness comes about and can be relieved. But they can only serve as a first step -- true, an indispensable first step -- toward the introduction to Freudian thought, for they were delivered before the development of the system took place. And while they give us, with some qualifications, a good historical account of the genesis and earlier formulation of psychoanalytic theory, they do not touch on the way Freud went on to use his discoveries about the disfunctioning of the mind in order to elucidate the genesis and fate of human culture. A restless, searching genius, prodigiously creative during a long life (1856-1938), Freud relentlessly thrust the probing searchlight of his basic discoveries about the mind into practically all the major aspects of man's activity. But in 1910, although then a fully mature thinker, Freud had ahead of him immense territories to explore.

The result of these explorations was a fairly systematic account of man and of his culture, with some undeveloped indications regarding man's relation to the universe. This is to say that Freud left us a system of philosophy of major proportions, and for us, men living in mid-century, a system as relevant as it is challenging and ambitious in its projected scope. It has this decisive advantage over the current existentialisms now so much in temporary vogue: it is not a reactionary movement, it accepts science; indeed, it claims that its basic hypotheses are scientifically derived and hence subject to scientific verification. Freud's system is not a finished system, in the sense Hegel's is; it is rather a comprehensive blueprint for an immense edifice whose already completed foundations rest on the rock of clinical data, and many of whose wings were left in a habitable stage of completion.

The reader who desires to become acquainted with Freud's thought would do well, after digesting these five lectures, to turn to the New Introductory Lectures on Psychoanalysis. What he should turn to after that depends altogether on his dominant interests. It is, however, indispensable to gain full familiarity with the Freudian analysis of the psyche and the way it functions, and it would also be advisable to acquire a sound acquaintance with the whole range of the system before turning to any one of its aspects for special study. But sooner or later the reader may want to become more deeply acquainted with, for instance, Freud's contributions to the treatment of mental illness; or he may want light on Freud's view of man's nature1 on his philosophical anthropology; or he may want knowledge of what is distinguishable but not separable from the latter, Freud's philosophy of culture, his views, that is to say, on religion, art and what in the English translation is called "civilization."

In any case, in whatever direction he turns, the reader can be certain that he is in for an exciting and a most rewarding adventure. Some readers will find the adventure shocking or even outrageous. But whatever their reactions, it would be well for them to bear in mind that a working knowledge of Freud is a necessary condition of being admitted to first-class citizenship in our world. No one today can gain without knowledge of Freud an adequate knowledge of aesthetics, literary or artistic criticism, sociology and certain recent developments in anthropology, and he cannot understand contemporary developments in the study of primitive religions, nor can he grasp contemporary trends in penology or child education.

The reason is simple: There are few, if any, humanistic disciplines that have not felt the impact of Freud's genius. It takes, therefore, a radically prejudiced mind to return from a serious study of Freud, not necessarily convinced of the truth of his doctrines, but unchanged by them. And I say, "it takes," and not "it would take," because one frequently runs into men of intelligence and learning, even men who plume themselves on their modernity, who display a granitic resistance to Freudian doctrine. That Freud sometimes goes out of his way to outrage his conventional reader no one can deny; that his views are shocking to the mid-Victorians among us, goes without saying; that he is in many important points in error can be shown to any one who is capable of argument; that he may have had an eroding effect on the American character is a point that can be argued with some plausibility; and that these objections do not at all exhaust the negative criticisms that can be leveled at Freud I would be the first to agree. But that they neutralize his contribution is a judgment that can be made only by a narrow and closed mind. Yet it must be owned that all too frequently Freud is rejected with an animus that exceeds in intensity our normal reactions to wrong or even to pernicious doctrines. The animus reminds one of the reaction of religious fanaticism to heresy, or of the Stalinists of the thirties to Trotskyites. It appears, therefore, to have its roots in deeply subjective soil. But whatever its source, it is as stubborn as it is purblind, and it is as implacable as it is uninformed. Within the same universe of discourse it can only be compared to the acceptance of Freudian doctrine one occasionally runs into even today: uncritical, unnecessarily touchy, partisan, closed.

It is possible to organize the body of Freudian doctrine in many ways. One can, for instance, assign various works to the several departments into which our university curriculum is divided. On such an organization the book on Leonardo would be assigned to one department, The Future of an Illusion to another, and so on with the rest. But the organization I find most useful for my purposes, already suggested above, is this: Freudian doctrine can be divided into a body of medical theory and a therapeutic technique, a philosophical anthropology, and a philosophy of culture. Of course, no such organization, no organization whatever, I dare say, of a mass of hypotheses of so heterogeneous a nature, although devised by as systematic a mind as that of Freud, would be fully adequate. This one is one I have found useful for my purposes; and my purposes are those of a student of philosophy.

But however we organize the Freudian works, the place to start from, if I may iterate an important point, is not susceptible of choice. It is fixed. All of Freud's doctrine flows from his basic and revolutionary insight into the way minds work or, more precisely, into the way they fail to work satisfactorily. Because its foundation is a theory of mind, we can say of Freudian philosophy that it represents a contemporary fulfillment of Hume's program to give an account of the whole of human experience in psychogenetic terms. There are significant differences, of course, as there are bound to be, given the time differences and the outlooks of the two thinkers. And the most important of these is that Hume started from an incredibly simplistic conception of the mind and of the way it enters into commerce with the world. Hume (and the so-called empirical tradition in which he is so influential a link) ignores mental forces that bring about the two-way interaction between the mind and the world. He ignores the creative way in which the mind enters as agent in the reception of external messages, in which it discerns values, and in which it construes moral decisions. He also ignores the way in which the affective matrix informs and transforms our grasp of the real world. But above all, for all his claims to being an empiricist, Hume's conception of the mind was an aprioristic one. If a defender of Hume retorts that he was after all a man of the eighteenth century and it is unfair to expect him to know what we know today, I reply that that may indeed be the case; but, unfortunately, among American and British philosophers he is not only an outstanding figure in the history of psychology and epistemology but he is still an operative influence of great power. Medicine in the 15th century was still being taught out of ancient texts of Galen. Today epistemologists and moral philosophers still go to Hume -- with results that need not be commented on. By contrast, Freud starts from a close observation of the mind. True, it is the sick mind he begins with; but it soon turns out that the difference between health and illness is less significant than it had been assumed to be prior to Freud. To ameliorate the derangements from which his patients suffered, Freud had to go beyond the surface and into the depths of the mind. And this put him, in one leap, way beyond the simplifications and reductions of eighteenth-century empiricists and contemporary academic psychologists and "empirical" philosophers.

Should it be objected that Freud did not do the job that he set out to do, it can be repeated that if he did not finish the vast enterprise, he laid down the lines along which the job was to be attempted. This is to say that Freud was able to devise a fairly comprehensive philosophical system. But he was able to do so, not simply because he was the discoverer of the unconscious, for he was not. We did not need Whyte's book on "The Unconscious Before Freud" to learn that the notion of the unconscious had its source at least in Leibniz, if not earlier. What Freud did was to show how the unconscious works, how drives are repressed and find satisfaction, and how sublimation creates culture. The upshot of his work has been as radical a revolution as we encounter in the history of thought. For Freud disclosed in conceptual terms what the poets had known all along in their own terms about the depth of the mind. But he went much farther than the poets, and it is simply to belittle his contribution to assume that all he did was to state in conceptual language what they had stated in mythopoetic terms. He offered a systematic account of what goes on beyond the range of our conscious observation. The information he came up with about the strategies and duplicities the mind employs to achieve ends which we do not let it pursue directly, and the account of the heavy burden of frustration which we must carry to become and remain human are, on first acquaintance, well nigh incredible. One remembers the comment Einstein is said to have made to a friend on returning one of Kafka's novels: Surely men can't be that complex. Surely, one says, that pathetic comedy that Freud offers us as a sober, scientific account of the way the mind works must have been concocted by a man who was as mad as he says we are. And this is a charge made seriously by some of his critics. But although Freud was no more free from neurotic traits than the rest of us, his was a ram-rod of a rationalistic mind, and what he discovered or claimed he discovered -- and this is where the value of his contribution ultimately lies — is susceptible of objective criticism and development.

Freud has been accused of being one of the leaders of the revolt against reason that no doubt is now going on. The neck of this old canard has so often been wrung that there is no point in doing it again. But Freud did indeed show that the control that we have assumed to have over ourselves is severely restricted, fragile and alarmingly undependable. If to disclose the nature of the facts makes a man responsible for them, meteorologists are to be blamed for the hurricanes they are trying to understand.

Let me iterate at the risk of annoying my reader that were it necessary radically to correct Freud's dynamic psychology today-a matter for specialists and not for amateurs -- the value of Freud's contribution would remain undiminished. For he stated a problem and offered a solution. If the solution is unacceptable, it can be corrected; if the problem was not correctly envisaged, it is also susceptible of reformulation. But once posed it can only be ignored by struthonian tricks, and these cannot be practiced when you are confronted with human beings that are suffering. As long, therefore, as we are burdened with the problem of mental illness we will have to remain grateful to Freud for the contribution he made. About the future, anyone's guess is as good as anyone else's; mine is that the time to forget Freud will come after the Angel blows the trumpet for the final judgment.

But what evidence did Freud offer for his bold speculations? Freud and his disciples have claimed that his hypotheses are scientific, in the sense in which the hypotheses of physicists or biologists are said to be scientific. This claim has been rejected by many philosophers on grounds that cannot be dismissed out of hand. Fortunately, it is not a quarrel whose merits need be examined here. It is enough to note that if we approach Freudian theory as philosophy, only an extreme anti-Freudian would deny that Freud starts with empirical data and elaborates his doctrines in the spirit of science, and not, as some philosophers do, in disregard of factual data and in a purely aprioristic way, or motivated, as are the philosophies of the Lebenswelt, by a more or less veiled dislike of science. Of course, it will also have to be acknowledged that when Freud undertakes speculatively to extrapolate the love and death drives beyond the psyche and turns them into cosmological principles, he is as little of an empiricist as was Empedocles. But Weltanschauungen are not meant to be scientific hypotheses nor are they iconic reproductions of reality. They are organizations of reality for purposes other than, as well as, the cognitive. And what Freud finally develops, starting from clinical data, is the project of a Weltanschauung.

Again, to acknowledge that Freud started from empirical data and developed his theories in the spirit of science is not to claim that he was a scientist. The claim cannot be effective for at least one reason (although there are others): "the spirit of science is an umbrella under which so many different modes of thought seek refuge that it hardly protects any of them. The denial, however, of scientific status to Freudian thought is done on the basis of rigoristic methodological criteria, said by positivist philosophers to be drawn from the physical sciences. Freud's theories certainly are not susceptible of the tests laid down by these criteria, and the efforts of psychoanalysts and philosophers of science friendly to psychoanalysis to prove that they are, seem to succeed only by relaxing the rigorism of the criteria. But why is it necessary to meet the attack on grounds chosen by the attackers? Why not challenge the assumptions underlying the positivist interpretation of science? This is not done because of the successful indoctrination carried on by the positivist philosophers according to whom there is only one philosophy of science, and that is their own.

While it is not possible to develop this point as fully as it deserves, one of the results of the application of the rigoristic criteria to all disciplines is worthy of note. It leads to the abandonment of all those problems that cannot be handled by methods that meet the criteria, however important and urgent, theoretically and practically, these problems may be. Thus in the pursuit of methodological respectability we are presented with quantified trivia and mountains of pseudo-rigorous observations of the obvious. These, often, add up to very little more than verified revelation of the fact, for instance, that the citizens of Middletown, a fair sample of whom have been canvassed, have been found to have five toes per foot; and that Duk-duks (or was it the Samoans?), when last visited by Margaret Mead, still had five toes per foot. This piece of knowledge, secured by The

Method of Science (in capitals and in the singular), is something we do not have a right to assert, whatever our hunches, until the results of the field research have been published, or, better still, until they have been confirmed by a second field count.

But if to deny scientific status to disciplines that do not meet the rigoristic criterion is to argue that none of these disciplines yields knowledge (on the assumption that only scientific knowledge is true knowledge), the reply to the denial contains two parts. The first is that these activities are concerned with important aspects of human life, which call for intellectual organization and understanding, whether Tom, Dick or Rudolph agree that the attention of which they are susceptible is cognitive in his sense or not. The second is that if only disciplines employing the methods of the positive sciences can be said to yield knowledge, we shall have to find a new term for what we formerly took to be the knowledge these non-scientific disciplines gave us and to which we now can no longer apply the term the positivists have kidnapped. The value of this verbal rearrangement, whatever it be, leaves the substantive issues exactly where they were before. Because the issue of the scientific status of Freud's theories is ultimately a quarrel between dogmatic rigorists on the one side and, on the other, middle of the road dogmatists concerned to be cut in on the prestige that the positive sciences enjoy in our epoch, let me take up the suggestion that we bypass the controversy and treat the Freudian system of thought as philosophy. If philosophy still deserves, as it has until now, the serious attention of some of the best minds that humanity has produced, or, to reduce the apology to minimal terms, if philosophy can be avoided only by the adoption of pure mindlessness (an impossible feat, even for some contemporary Kierkegaardians), then Freudian theory deserves the same kind of attention that the theories of the recognized philosophers deserve, and for the very same reasons.

But -- I hear some of my readers object -- isn't your approach an absurd innovation? The author of "Totem and Taboo" -- with its archaic anthropology -- Moses and Monotheism, The Future of an Illusion, Civilization and Its Discontents and a few other works of this kind may no doubt be called a philosopher. After all, the word has no single, well-defined acceptation, and you have as much right to call Freud a philosopher as Lear the King had to call the mad beggar a "learned Theban." But this loose use of the world "philosopher" -- the objector continues -- overlooks a fact you yourself have emphasized, namely, that Freud accomplished what he did because he was a psychoanalyst, and all of his thinking had its source in, and was controlled by, the exigencies of clinical experience.

I reply that the facts on which the objection is based cannot be rejected, but the interpretation put on them is nevertheless inadmissible. It is not a thinker's point of departure, nor even the equipment with which he begins his inquiry, that gives him the right to the title of philosopher. He has a right to it because of the manner in which he carries on his inquiry. And it may well be that Freud's philosophic speculations will constitute, in the long run, his most lasting contribution to the history of thought. They may, let me say it again, be his most lasting contribution, not in the sense that his conclusions will be accepted as truth without revision, but in the sense that they will retain their hold on thought when his therapeutic technique will be of interest solely to the historian of clinical psychology. It is true that he has a secure place in the history of medicine. The revolution he brought about forced a turn in the treatment of mental illness that is irreversible. If he had done no more than force recognition of the seriousness of the problem of mental illness and broadened and deepened our awareness of the fact that the problem touches not only utterly broken down patients but touches a much larger segment of the population, if he had done no more than arouse in us a sense of the urgent need to develop satisfactory means of treating mental disorders, Freud would have earned the place he securely occupies in medicine's Hall of Fame. But these claims do not exhaust his contribution. Nevertheless, it may well turn out that the techniques devised by Freud for therapeutic treatment may gradually become obsolete. This is a constant and indeed desirable occurrence in the history of science, technology and the applied arts. Should it happen to psychoanalysis, Freud will be remembered in history, but he will also be recognized in the future as the philosopher that I am urging he is.

This suggestion is not put forth as a prediction, and it is advanced with the utmost diffidence. So far as I know, only Marxists have a scientific crystal ball. For us who do not have such means of looking into the future, is there anything more silly than to take historical predictions seriously? But there are signs that psychoanalysis, as therapeutic technique does not have a rosy future. The grounds for this judgment are these: Psychoanalytic treatment was developed by Freud, as he makes clear in this little book, because at the time of its origin physicians could not find physical sources in the brain or the nervous system for the disorders they were called upon to treat. So far as it could then be discovered, patients with sound constitutions nevertheless became mentally ill. In the light of the best knowledge available when Freud began the use of psychoanalysis, therefore, no alternative was open but to assume that mental disorders had their origin in the mind itself.

But this is tantamount to assuming the autonomy of psychology. Note in passing that the assumption is in conflict with Freud's commitment to nineteenth-century materialism. In any case, the autonomy of psychoanalysis is put in question by recent developments in the treatment of mental illness through drugs and by reported discoveries that point to the fact that some mental disorders seem to be correlated with glandular and other types of somatic malfunctioning. We cannot blame Freud, of course, for not knowing when he began his career what is known today. The success of psychoanalysis and the then available knowledge -- or more exactly, the lack of it -- suggested that the source of mental disorders was the mind itself. But he never faced the difficulties in which his position involved him. What Freud was up against was the old mind-body problem. Freud spent a good deal of time on what he called his "research"-a term, apparently, which he applied to his purely speculative activity, much of it beyond relevance to the narrow exigencies of therapy. And yet he never wrestled seriously with the mind-body problem. Even if we grant the truth of the Freudian theory, its acceptance does not commit us to the belief that it is a body of hypotheses free from foundational defects. Its failure of awareness as regards the mind-body problem is one of its most serious defects, and it is one that recent developments force on our attention with an urgency that it did not have before.

What do Freud or his disciples have to say on the relation of mind to body? The little we can find on the subject is utterly inadequate. There are no books by psychoanalysts to compare with such works as Analysis of Mind, The Nature of Thought, or The Concept of Mind. While committed to the autonomy of psychology, Freud was certain that there was some sort of connection between mind and body, such that the former drew its energy from the latter. And he even offered us a substitute for the pineal gland of Cartesian fame, when in all seriousness he told us that the drives or instincts fill the id with energy drawn from somatic sources. But these instincts are apparently hybrid, now vaguely thought of as physical, now as psychic, and he does not seem to have been seriously aware of the difficulties with which they present us.

The claim, at any rate, is that mental energy has physical sources. This is, of course, old hat, but the problems that this kind of assertion brings with it are equally old hat. How are somatic processes transformed into mental excitations? Again, isn't the notion of mental energy, repeatedly used by Freud, an amputated metaphor, so to speak, whose vehicle is clear enough but whose tenor is not available for inspection? Freud, of course, for all his deep-rooted nineteenth-century materialism, could not go with the behaviorists. He could not call a neurosis a ghost in a machine. Psychological malformations, when you have to treat them, cannot be considered mere ghosts. Or if they can, it turns out that ghosts have an obdurate reality. But how can any one be confident that the neuroses originate in the psyche when one faces the fact that Freud dealt with this problem in as cavalier a manner as he did? He tells us that the source of the excitations created by the drives in the id is the body. It looks as if he were working both sides of the street. A nineteenth-century materialist had developed a technique of therapy and a theory that contradicted his materialistic faith. It is not enough to tell us that the drives arise from sources of stimulation within the body. Nor do the candor and intellectual integrity expressed in Freud's happy phrase, that the theory of the instincts is the mythology of psychoanalysis, enable him to dispose of the troublesome questions that he so lightly sought to dispose of with his quip. A felicitous phrase will push the problem out of sight for the uncritical. But sooner or later the problem will rear its obstinate head, and it does so now, when we can no longer ignore the fact that some neuroses have been relieved, and human beings have been returned to useful lives, by physical therapy.

Some Freudians have attempted to meet the challenge by arguing that while the new treatments may relieve the symptoms, they do not get at their root. But this retort will not do, for it is based on the assumption that the mind is indeed the source of its own disorders, and it is precisely this assumption that the success of drug therapy and glandular research puts in question. And I do not say, solves; I say merely, puts in question. Further, it fails to meet the very serious arguments of behaviorists such as Eysenck, who argue that the neurosis is nothing else than the symptoms, and not a thing or condition lying somewhere behind them or underneath them. One need not side with the behaviorist in order to conclude that however the psychoanalyst chooses to solve it, he is confronted by a formidable problem. For he cannot both assert the autonomy of psychology -- even if he only asserts it by implication-and be, as Ruth Munroe says Freud was, "biologically oriented."

In due humility it should be acknowledged that until this puzzle is satisfactorily solved the dogmatic stances so frequently taken by psychologists and philosophers ill befit the inquiring mind. Subjectivists yearning for immortality, laboratory behaviorists attempting to solve philosophical problems they are not equipped to handle and philosophical behaviorists exorcising ghosts from machines by sprinkling them with verbal holy water --each and every one of them has his solution. But in fact the problem does not seem to be nearer solution today than it was when Descartes or Spinoza tackled it. In any case, were the problem to remain where it is today or were it even to be solved overnight, the clinician qua clinician need not be a theoretical apparatchik. His professional concern is to get his patient to function more or less normally -- that is to say, to enable him to get by, to meet more or less adequately the demands of a given environment. But if a mental disorder can be treated by physical means, or in so far as it can be, it may be expected that psychoanalysis as a therapeutic technique will recede in importance. All the more since psychoanalysts have not been able to meet the challenge -- an old one, but one that is being pressed today vigorously by a number of critics -- to the effect that there are no available statistics to show that they are as successful with their techniques as ordinary physicians are. Not only do we know the cause of tetanus, but we can also control it with relative success. And when environmental conditions permit, yellow fever can be checked. And polio vaccine works. But knowledge that psychoanalysis is effective, in the hard sense of the term "knowledge," we simply do not have.

This then is the reason we may raise the question as to the future of psychoanalysis as a therapeutic technique. And this is also the reason for my urging that the contribution made by Freudian theory to philosophy may be recognized in the future. It should be noted that it is only recently, as such things go, that philosophers have begun to wake up to the challenge of Freud. As a rule, American and English philosophers of my generation, and a fortiori, of an older generation, simply were not aware of Freud as a philosophical force, or, when they were, did not come seriously to grips with his views. The tendency was to dismiss him out of hand. I once heard Morris Cohen earnestly say that the notion of unconscious ideas was a contradiction in terms, which, of course, made it nonsense.

There were no doubt reasons for the silent treatment that Freud received from the philosophers. The claims psychoanalysts made that their hypotheses meet the demands of scientific method cannot be defended. But what is much more serious, as the above remarks on the mind-body problem show, is that viewed philosophically Freud's ideas are crude. But the help Freud can give some philosophers and the challenge his views constitute for others are there, if not from the very beginning of Freudian thought, at least from, let us say, 1915, when it may be said that Freud began his meta-psychological writing. The crudeness of the theory does not justify our ignoring it. Were philosophers to decide that they should pay attention only to perfect theories, they would do well to pack up and go fishing till Kingdom Come.

But how can a body of doctrine which is admittedly coarse be of help or be a challenge to the professional philosopher? What can men equipped with exacting standards, who demand tightly woven thought, who insist on coherence, clarity and precision of language, get from a man who frivolously calls one of his basic assumptions his mythology? The answer is that they can get a great deal, if they remember that philosophers are, first of all, men whose business it is to look for trouble, and that they look for trouble in their own work before they look for it in the work of their colleagues. Philosophy is philosophizing. Its task is the search. And if part of its reward, and a most important part at that, is the illusion of finding a nugget of truth after a hard day's panning, that illusion, alas, is as ephemeral as it is ill-founded. Even as he feasts his eyes on his find, in his heart he knows that he will soon put it aside to begin his work again. The imperfections of his find urge him on. The philosopher is lured by the hope that tomorrow, or the day after, he will find what he is after. This hopeless hope urges him to further effort. Such a man does not much care where he searches. And for that reason, fully aware of the philosophical defects of Freud's thought, he nevertheless finds Freudian ideas of inestimable value.

But precisely in what sense? Let me give a few instances of the help or challenge that the philosopher gets or can get from Freud. A few specific examples will do more than a general consideration to express what I have in mind. But let me reiterate that what the philosopher is looking for is not finished truth. What he looks for are challenges, fruitful questions that peremptorily demand answers. Consider, then, as a first example, one of the challenges that many American and English philosophers are confronted by when they read Freud. Contemporary American and English philosophers are naturalists by faith.

This means that they believe that nature is all there is, and that it is therefore not necessary to invent factors external to it in order to account for any of its processes or parts. But how do we know nature? We look at it, we know it by means of experience. Experience and nothing but experience is the source of knowledge. But what is experience except the process of employing our senses and systematizing what we gather through them? To pass muster, therefore, knowledge must be made up of statements that can be certified by experience. This is not true of mathematics and logic, but the empiricist points out that neither of these two disciplines refers to the world, and they need not pass the tests that empirical knowledge must meet.

Much else is included in naturalism besides the fideistic tenet as to the all-inclusiveness of nature and the way to know it. Among others, two important articles should be mentioned in passing. The first is the naturalist's claim that his philosophy is utterly free of faith. The second is a tenet so widely spread and so deeply rooted in our philosophical world that it calls for a modicum of truculence and foolhardiness even to point to it. The tenet may be loosely called our contemporary nominalistic orthodoxy. A man who seriously asserts that value has ontic status is an intellectual clod-hopper and unfit for the company of twentieth-century philosophers. It should also be noted that naturalism is not a "school" of philosophy, in the sense that the idealisms of the nineteenth century or the various existentialisms or phenomenology's of the twentieth century are "schools." Rather, it is a temper of mind and a methodological commitment, a way of cutting the universe down to size in order to manage it by methods that have succeeded in the sciences and that, it is hoped, will succeed, at least to some extent, in philosophy.

It should not be surprising, therefore, that naturalists are all enthusiastic evolutionists. But their philosophical enthusiasm carries them beyond biology. In this, of course, they are not alone. Be that as it may; they espouse the doctrine that man and his institutions evolved from a lower form of life, from some higher ape. As the distinguished anthropologist Mr. Carleton Coon would have it, man comes from a monkey who gave up swinging from the branches and took to the ground in order to turn stones in search of bugs to eat. I forget exactly how the story goes, but I seem to remember that the forest was shrinking and eggs were in short supply. Anyhow that's how we came about. But how did man come by his notion of right and wrong? By his recognition of beauty? By his reverence for the holy? By his respect for the truth? I have examined Mr. Coon's answers to these questions elsewhere. Here all I need to say, much as I hate to say it, is that they put a man of unchallengeable scientific stature on the plane with the prudish grandmother who invented the story about the stork. But how does the philosopher who is a naturalist answer these questions? A scientist need not answer them: he shrugs his shoulders and admits he does not know. But a philosopher who asserts he knows that nature is all-inclusive cannot shrug his shoulders. If he has no answer for them, he must acknowledge that a modernized version of that old ghost, the missing link, has done his faith in. Only it's not bones that are missing: the museums are full of them, some of them planted by jokers. What we need to know is how man came by those virtues that make him human.

Before Franz Boas put an end to their yarn-spinning, anthropologists and philosophers had a lot of fun concocting stories as to how man created the institutions that marked the rise from his brute ancestors. After Boas called them to order, yarn spinning became unfashionable, unless it was done, as Mr. Coon does it, for the benefit of the intellectually unwashed. The questions, however, that the old storytellers sought to answer with their tales have not disappeared. They are still with us. What has happened is that by tacit agreement, naturalists have decided not to face them. What it amounts to is a conspiracy of silence -- unconscious, but effective nevertheless. I am not sure what the logic is behind the conspiracy, but it seems to add up to something like this: "If we choose not to see the trouble, it isn't there." This is a struthonian philosophy in splendiferous triumph. But philosophical questions are not nullified when philosophers take to playing ostrich.

When naturalistic philosophers turn to these critical questions what they offer us is totally inadequate. Thus we find Santayana assuring us that all ideal developments have a natural basis. But this is a mere assertion unless we are told by what processes, by the employment of what virtues, man came to create his institutions. To these questions all the naturalist can reply is that if they are ideal components of experience, they have a natural basis. And this is an answer, I need not call to the reader's attention, that is not worth the cost of the ribbon with which it is typed. Or they have another answer. They tell us that the distinctly human faculties emerged. With this verbal fig leaf they cover or think they cover the shame of their ignorance. But either emergence is a verbal fig leaf, or it is an appeal to miracle. And neither of the two devices is one that any one who takes science seriously can employ with self respect.

It is at this point that Freud can offer help to the naturalist. Freud offers him an account, in both philogenetic and ontogenetic terms, as to the way distinctly human institutions and values came about. Morality, religion, art, culture in general, are the product of processes that Freud found -- or so he tells us -- operative in human living. They all are, therefore, natural. These Freudian accounts, admissible or inadmissible as they may be found to be, are a challenge if not a help to the naturalist, for if he accepts them, he has added a badly needed link in a system of explanation that in principle should be continuous from simple beginnings to complex end terms; and if he rejects them, the minimal credit he must give Freud is that the latter led him to face a problem that he had until then either ignored or overlooked, but one without a solution to which his theory became an elaborate begging of the question. But more is due Freud than minimal credit. For a man who puts forth a hypothesis, if he does not offer us something that is acceptable, at least offers us something that can be criticized and from which, upon correcting it, we can go on to further inquiry.

I am not asserting that the Freudian theories of the origin of morality, art, religion and culture in general are acceptable. I have put in print my reasons for rejecting Freud's hypothesis of the origin of morality, and I have more than a hunch that an examination of Freud's account of the origin of art, religion and culture in general would uncover defects that would make them unacceptable. All I am asserting is that because Freud wrestles with problems that naturalists should be concerned with, he can be of help to them or constitute for them a challenge.

If this were the only way in which Freud could help or challenge the naturalist, it would be sufficient to hold him in respect. But there are other reasons for so holding him. Take as a second instance the way in which Freudian doctrine challenges moral philosophers. I do not mean meta-ethicists; I mean philosophers concerned with substantive questions of morality. Again, let me put the matter in concrete terms. Philosophers of diverse orientation have held, in varying ways and for different reasons, that moral decisions involve knowledge, and not merely knowledge of the probable consequences of our acts, but knowledge of the intentions back of them, which is to say, self-knowledge.

Thus, for Santayana the life of reason is achieved when we survey our desires and devise a project according to which the maximum number of desires can be fulfilled in harmony. For such a view, one would expect lucidity about one's self is of paramount importance. And this is indeed true of Santayana's philosophy. Lucidity is a virtue that is highly praised by him. But it is the very possibility of the self-knowledge that is the foundation of the life of reason that Freud challenges. Self-knowledge is not merely a matter of honesty, courage and the ability to turn our gaze inward with some persistence. These virtues will carry us some of the way, but not too far. Self-knowledge does not come that easily. And Santayana himself is quite a nice illustration of the insufficiency of his vaunted lucidity. He thought he had achieved lucidity because he acknowledged to himself his sexual eccentricity. But he was utterly self-deceived. We know enough about the type of neurosis from which he suffered to hold, with a modicum of confidence, that his vaunted lucidity constituted the very means by which he avoided facing the probable fact that homosexuality is a form of illness, and not, as some homosexuals claim, a way of life as desirable as heterosexuality. Nor is Santayana the only man to employ lucidity as a strategy of self-deception. For Gide, sincerity was a high virtue. But the specific difficulties of men like Santayana and Gide aside, if the life of reason depends for its successful realization on knowledge of one's self as well as probable knowledge of the consequences of one's actions, it can be no more than a very imperfectly attainable ideal, and Santayana's criticisms of pre-rational and post-rational morality lose their sting.

What I have said about Santayana's conception of the good life applies, with the necessary modifications, to Dewey's account of the way in which moral problems are solved morally. It also applies to the moral philosophies of such writers as Warner Fite. It holds indeed for any moral philosophy that makes self-knowledge one of the essential conditions of the moral life. For what we can know about ourselves and our desires without the psychoanalyst's aid is meager and superficial. If Freud is right about the self, the strategies we successfully employ to deceive ourselves are the highest evidence of our superiority over the brutes and, to top the irony, the basis of our distinctively human achievements.

But note again that I am not asserting that Freud is right about the ineradicable difficulties in the way of self-knowledge. All that need be asserted is that he presents some moral philosophers with a challenge that cannot be ignored.

Let me cite another instance of Freud's challenge to the philosopher. From certain quarters we hear a great deal of talk about man's freedom. Man is said to be free, and the statement is said not to call for qualification. But there is no denying that neuroses limit human freedom. And Freudians seem to be right in their belief that no man is utterly devoid of neuroses. In what sense can we say that man is free, if we believe he is? And if we deny it, in what sense can we ascribe meaningful responsibility to the individual?

I am not suggesting that this problem has its source in Freudian psychology. But I do suggest that Freud forces a theoretical formulation of it which is different from what has been generally accepted until now, and that Freud imparts to the problem a practical urgency that it lost when the problem ceased to be viewed in a theological context. It is no longer a question of either-or, but of more or less, and this makes it more difficult. Again, it is not an abstract problem, to be discussed in the class room, as to whether and in what sense man can be said to be free, but other-wise leaving us exactly where we were before we took a course in philosophy. It is now a question of determinable factors operative in specific syndromes. The Freudian challenge returns the question to the status it had in the days of Calderon, when in Spain (and the same thing happened in Holland at about the same time) there were riots in the streets over predestination as there were in Byzantium over a critical vowel. The philosophical problem has engaged philosophers all along. But the responsibility demanded of us as ordinary citizens was not altered. Freud, however, has changed all that. In the light of his theory the term "insane" must be relegated to the historical dictionary where we find terms like "brain fever" and the famous "phlogiston." But more important, the increasing introduction of psychological considerations in the courtroom not only increases the practical difficulties of arriving at justice, but underlines a fact practical men tend to overlook, namely, that what goes on in the courtroom is intimately dependent on philosophical issues of major dimensions and of an order of difficulty which is appalling.

These considerations are far from exhausting the way Freud impinges or should impinge on the philosopher's dogmatic siesta. But they are sufficient to convince those who have an open mind that Freud has a place among the philosophers, or at any rate, that they cannot afford to ignore him. There are many reasons for considering him one of the profoundly revolutionary minds of our modern world. When one learns to move in the world of Freud one sees that there are better and more reasons for coupling his name with that of Copernicus and Darwin than the one he advanced. He claimed that his views constituted the third great outrage to man's self-respect. Perhaps they did. But he has done more than outrage us -- as the other two did, of course. He has led us to a knowledge of ourselves and of culture that our ancestors did not possess. And this judgment as to our debt to him holds whether one accepts his hypotheses as he formulated them, or whether one rejects them. For in the latter case, unless we choose to join the ostriches, we are forced to seek better solutions of his problems than those he proposed.

ELISEO VIVAS

THE ORIGIN AND DEVELOPMENT OF PSYCHOANALYSIS

First Lecture

Ladies and Gentlemen: It is a new and somewhat embarrassing experience for me to appear as lecturer before students of the New World. I assume that I owe this honor to the association of my name with the theme of psychoanalysis, and consequently it is of psychoanalysis that I shall aim to speak. I shall attempt to give you in very brief form an historical survey of the origin and further development of this new method of research and cure.

Granted that it is a merit to have created psychoanalysis, it is not my merit. I was a student, busy with the passing of my last examinations, when another physician of Vienna, Dr. Joseph Breuer, made the first application of this method to the case of an hysterical girl (1880-82). We must now examine the history of this case and its treatment, which can be found in detail in "Studien uber Hysterie," later published by Dr. Breuer and myself.

But first one word. I have noticed, with considerable satisfaction, that the majority of my hearers do not belong to the medical profession. Now do not fear that a medical education is necessary to follow what I shall have to say. We shall now accompany the doctors a little way, but soon we shall take leave of them and follow Dr. Breuer on a way which is quite his own.

Dr. Breuer's patient was a girl of twenty-one, of a high degree of intelligence. She had developed in the course of her two years' illness a series of physical and mental disturbances which well deserved to be taken seriously. She had a severe paralysis of both right extremities, with anesthesia, and at times the same affection of the members of the left side of the body, disturbance of eye-movements, and much impairment of vision; difficulty in maintaining the position of the head, an intense *Tussis nervosa*, nausea when she attempted to take nourishment, and at one time for several weeks a loss of the power to drink, in spite of tormenting thirst. Her power of speech was also diminished, and this progressed so far that she could neither speak: nor understand her mother tongue; and, finally, she was subject to states of "absence," of confusion, delirium, alteration of her whole personality. These states will later claim our attention.

When one hears of such a case, one does not need to be a physician to incline to the opinion that we are concerned here with a serious injury, probably of the brain, for which there is little hope of cure and which will probably lead to the early death of the patient. The doctors will tell us, however, that in one type of cases with just as unfavorable symptoms, another, far more favorable, opinion is justified. When one finds such a series of symptoms in the case of a young girl whose vital organs (heart, kidneys) are shown by objective tests to be normal, but who has suffered from strong emotional disturbances, and when the symptoms differ in certain finer characteristics from what one might logically expect, in a case like this the doctors are not too much disturbed. They consider that there is present no organic lesion of the brain, but that enigmatical state, known since the time of the Greek physicians as hysteria, which can simulate a whole series of symptoms of various diseases. They consider in such a case that the life of the patient is not in danger and that a restoration to health will probably come about of itself. The differentiation of such an hysteria from a severe organic lesion is not always very easy. But we do not need to know how a differential diagnosis of this kind is made; you may be sure that the case of Breuer's patient was such that no skillful physician could fail to diagnose an hysteria. We may also add a word here from the history of the case. The illness first appeared while the patient was caring for her father, whom she tenderly loved, during the severe illness which led to his death, a task which she was compelled to abandon because she herself fell ill.

So far it has seemed best to go with the doctors, but we shall soon part company with them. You must not think that the outlook of a patient with regard to medical aid is essentially bettered when the diagnosis points to hysteria rather than organic disease of the brain. Against the serious brain diseases medical skill is in most cases powerless, but also in the case of hysterical affections the doctor can do nothing. He must leave it to benign nature, when and how his hopeful prognosis will be realized.[1] Accordingly, with the recognition of the disease as hysteria, little is changed in the situation of the patient, but there is a great change in the attitude of the doctor. We can observe that he acts quite differently toward hystericals than toward patients suffering from organic diseases. He will not bring the same interests to the former as to the latter, since their suffering is much less serious and yet seems to set up the claim to be valued just as seriously.

But there is another motive in this action. The physician, who through his studies has learned so much that is hidden from the laity, can realize in his

---

[1] I know that this view no longer holds today, but in the lecture I take myself and my hearers back to the time before 1880. If things have become different since that time it has been largely due to the work the history of which I am sketching.

thought the causes and alterations of the brain disorders in patients suffering from apoplexy or dementia, a representation which must be right up to a certain point, for by it he is enabled to understand the nature of each symptom. But before the details of hysterical symptoms, all his knowledge, his anatomical-physiological and pathological education, desert him. He cannot understand hysteria. He is in the same position before it as the layman. And that is not agreeable to anyone who is in the habit of setting such a high valuation upon his knowledge. Hystericals, accordingly, to lose his sympathy; he considers them persons who overstep the laws of his science, as the orthodox regard heretics; he ascribes to them all possible evils, blames them for exaggeration and intentional deceit, "simulation," and he punishes them by withdrawing his interest.

Now Dr. Breuer did not deserve this reproach in this case; he gave his patient sympathy and interest, although at first he did not understand how to help her. Probably this was easier for him on account of those superior qualities of the patient's mind and character, to which he bears witness in his account of the case.

His sympathetic observation soon found the means which made the first help possible. It had been noticed that the patient, in her states of "absence," of psychic alteration, usually mumbled over several words to herself. These seemed to spring from associations with which her thoughts were busy. The doctor, who was able to get these words, put her in a sort of hypnosis and repeated them to her over and over, in order to bring up any associations that they might have. The patient yielded to his suggestion and reproduced for him those psychic creations which controlled her thoughts during her "absences," and which betrayed themselves in these single spoken words. These were fancies, deeply sad, often poetically beautiful, day dreams, we might call them, which commonly took as their starting point the situation of a girl beside the sickbed of her father. Whenever she had related a number of such fancies, she was, as it were, freed and restored to her normal mental life. This state of health could last for several hours, and then give place on the next day to a new "absence," which was removed in the same way by relating the newly created fancies. It was impossible not to get the impression that the psychic alteration which was expressed in the "absence1' was a consequence of the excitations originating from these intensely emotional fancy images. The patient herself, who at this time of her illness strangely enough understood and spoke only English, gave this new kind of treatment the name "talking cure," or jokingly designated it as "chimney-sweeping."

The doctor soon hit upon the fact that through such cleansing of the soul more could be accomplished than a temporary removal of the constantly recurring mental "clouds." Symptoms of the disease would disappear when in hypnosis the patient could be made to remember the situation and the associative connections under which they first appeared, provided free vent was given to the emotions which they aroused. "There was in the summer a time of intense heat, and the patient had suffered very much from thirst; for, without any apparent reason, she had suddenly become unable to drink. She would take a glass of water in her hand, but as soon as it touched her lips she would push it away as though suffering from hydrophobia. Obviously for these few seconds she was in her absent state. She ate only fruit, melons and the like, in order to relieve this tormenting thirst. When this had been going on about six weeks, she was talking one day in hypnosis about her English governess, whom she disliked, and finally told, with every sign of disgust, how she bad come into the room of the governess, and how that lady's little dog, that she abhorred, had drunk out of a glass. Out of respect for the conventions the patient had remained silent. Now, after she had given energetic expression to her restrained anger, she asked for a drink, drank a large quantity of water without trouble, and woke from hypnosis with the glass at her lips. The symptom thereupon vanished permanently."

Permit me to dwell for a moment on this experience. No one had ever cured an hysterical symptom by such means before, or had come so near understanding its cause. This would be a pregnant discovery if the expectation could be confirmed that still other, perhaps the majority of symptoms, originated in this way and could be removed by the same method. Breuer spared no pains to convince himself of this and investigated the pathogenesis of the other more serious symptoms in a more orderly way. Such was indeed the case; almost all the symptoms originated in exactly this way, as remnants, as precipitates. If you like, of affectively toned experiences, which for that reason we later called "psychic traumata." The nature of the symptoms became clear through their relation to the scene which caused them. They were, to use the technical term, "determined" (*determiniert*) by the scene whose memory traces they embodied, and so could no longer be described as arbitrary or enigmatical functions of the neurosis.

Only one variation from what might be expected must be mentioned. It was not always a single experience which occasioned the symptom, but usually several, perhaps many similar, repeated traumata cooperated in this effect. It was necessary to repeat the whole series of pathogenic memories in chronological sequence, and of course in reverse order, the last first and the first last. It was quite impossible to reach the first and often most essential trauma directly, without first clearing away those coming later.

You will of course want to hear me speak of other examples of the causation of hysterical symptoms beside this of inability to drink on account of the disgust caused by the dog drinking from the glass. I must, however, if I hold to my program, limit myself to very few examples. Breuer relates, for instance, that his patient's visual disturbances could be traced back to external causes, in the following way: "The patient, with tears in her eyes, was sitting by the sickbed when her father suddenly asked her what time it was. She could not see distinctly, strained her eyes to see, brought the watch near her eyes so that the dial seemed very large (macropia and strabismus conv.), or else she tried hard to suppress her tears, so that the sick man might not see them."

All the pathogenic impressions sprang from the time when she shared in the care of her sick father. "Once she was watching at night in the greatest anxiety for the patient, who was in a high fever, and in suspense, for a surgeon was expected from Vienna, to operate on the patient. Her mother had gone out for a little while, and Anna sat by the sickbed, her right arm hanging over the back of her chair. She fell into a revery and saw a black snake emerge, as it were, from the wall and approach the sick man as though to bite him. (It is very probable that several snakes had actually been seen in the meadow behind the house, that she had already been frightened by them, and that these former experiences furnished the material for the hallucination.) She tried to drive off the creature, but was as though paralyzed. Her right arm, which was hanging over the back of the chair, had 'gone to sleep,' become anaesthetic and paretic, and as she was looking at it, the fingers changed into little snakes with death's-heads. (The nails.) Probably she attempted to drive away the snake with her paralyzed right hand, and so the anesthesia and paralysis of this member formed associations with the snake hallucination. When this had vanished, she tried in her anguish to speak, but could not. She could not express herself in any language, until finally she thought of the words of an English nursery song, and thereafter she could think and speak only in this language." When the memory of this scene was revived in hypnosis the paralysis of the right arm, which had existed since the beginning of the illness, was cured and the treatment ended.

When, a number of years later, began to use Breuer's researches and treatment on my own patients, my experiences completely coincided with his. In the case of a woman of about forty, there was a tic, a peculiar smacking noise which manifested itself whenever she was laboring under any excitement, without any obvious cause. It had its origin in two experiences which had this common element, that she attempted to make no noise, but that by a sort of counter-will this noise broke the stillness. On the first occasion, she had finally after much trouble put her sick child to sleep, and she tried to be very quiet so as not to awaken it. On the second occasion, during a ride with both her children in a thunderstorm the horses took fright, and she carefully avoided any noise for fear of frightening them still more. I give this example instead of many others which are cited in the *Studien uber Hysterie*.

Ladies and Gentlemen, if you will permit me to generalize, as is indispensable in so brief a presentation, we may express our results up to this point in the formula: *Our hysterical patients suffer from reminiscences. Their symptoms are the remnants and the memory symbols of certain (traumatic) experiences.*

A comparison with other memory symbols from other sources will perhaps enable us better to understand this symbolism. The memorials and monuments, with which we adorn our great cities, are also such memory symbols. If you walk through London you will find before one of the greatest railway stations of the city a richly decorated Gothic pillar -- "Charing Cross." One of the old Plantagenet kings, in the thirteenth century, caused the body of his beloved queen Eleanor to be borne to Westminster, and had Gothic crosses erected at each of the stations where the coffin was sent down. Charing Cross is the last of these monuments, which preserve the memory of this sad journey. In another part of the city, you will see a high pillar of more modern construction, which is merely called "the Monument." This is in memory of the great fire which broke out in the neighborhood in the year 1666, and destroyed a great part of the city. These monuments are memory symbols like the hysterical symptoms; so far the comparison seems justified. But what would you say to a Londoner who today stood sadly before the monument to the funeral of Queen Eleanor, instead of going about his business with the haste engendered by modern industrial conditions, or rejoicing with the young queen of his own heart? Or to another, who before "the Monument" bemoaned the burning of his loved native city, which long since has arisen again so much more splendid than before?

Now hystericals and all neurotics behave like these two unpractical Londoners, not only in that they remember the painful experiences of the distant past, but because they are still strongly affected by them. They cannot escape from the past and neglect present reality in its favor. This fixation of the mental life on the pathogenic traumata is an essential, and practically a most significant characteristic of the neurosis. I will willingly concede the objection, which you are probably formulating, as you think over the history of Breuer's patient. All her traumata originated at the time when she was caring for her sick father, and her symptoms could only be regarded as memory symbols of his sickness and death. They corresponded to mourning, and a fixation on thoughts of the dead so short a time after death is certainly not pathological, but rather corresponds to normal emotional behavior. I concede this: there is nothing abnormal in the fixation of feeling on the trauma shown by Breuer's patient. But in other cases, like that of the tic that I have mentioned, the occasions for which lay ten and fifteen years back, the characteristic of this abnormal clinging to the past is very clear, and Breuer's patient would probably have developed it, if she had not come under the 'cathartic treatment" such a short time after the traumatic experiences and the beginning of the disease.

We have so far only explained the relation of the hysterical symptoms to the life history of the patient; now by considering two further factors which Breuer observed, we may get a hint as to the processes of the beginning of the illness and those of the cure. With regard to the first, it is especially to be noted that Breuer's patient in almost all pathogenic situations had to suppress a strong excitement, instead of giving vent to it by appropriate words and deeds. In the little experience with her governess' dog, she suppressed, through regard for the conventions, all manifestations of her very intense disgust. While she was seated by her father's sickbed, she was careful to betray nothing of her anxiety and her painful depression to the patient. When, later, she reproduced the same scene before the physician, the emotion which she had suppressed on the occurrence of the scene burst out with especial strength, as though it had been pent up all along. The symptom which had been caused by that scene reached its greatest intensity while the doctor was striving to revive the memory of the scene, and vanished after it had been fully laid bare. On the other hand, experience shows that if the patient is reproducing the traumatic scene to the physician, the process has no curative effect if, by some peculiar chance, there is no development of emotion. It is apparently these emotional processes upon which the illness of the patient and the restoration to health are dependent. We feel justified in regarding "emotion" as a quantity which may become increased, derived and displaced. So we are forced to the conclusion that the patient fell ill because the emotion developed in the pathogenic situation was prevented from escaping normally, and that the essence of the sickness lies in the fact that these "imprisoned" (*eingeklemmt*) emotions undergo a series of abnormal changes. In part they are preserved as a lasting charge and as a source of constant disturbance in psychical life; in part they undergo a change into unusual bodily innervations and inhibitions, which present themselves as the physical symptoms of the case. We have coined the name "hysterical conversion" for the latter process. Part of our mental energy is, under normal conditions, conducted off by way of physical innervation and gives what we call "the expression of emotions." Hysterical conversion exaggerates this part of the course of a mental process which is emotionally colored; it corresponds to a far more intense emotional expression, which finds outlet by new paths. If a stream flows into two channels, an overflow of one will take place as soon as the current in the other meets with an obstacle.

You see that we are in a fair way to arrive at a purely psychological theory of hysteria, in which we assign the first rank to the affective processes. A second observation of Breuer compels us to ascribe to the altered condition of consciousness a great part in determining the characteristics of the disease. His patient showed many sorts of mental states, conditions of "absence," confusion and alteration of character, besides her normal state. In her normal state she was entirely ignorant of the pathogenic scenes and of their connection with her symptoms. She had forgotten those scenes, or at any rate had dissociated them from their pathogenic connection. When the patient was hypnotized, it was possible, after considerable difficulty; to recall those scenes to her memory, and by this means of recall the symptoms were removed. It would have been extremely perplexing to know how to interpret this fact, if hypnotic practice and experiments had not pointed out the way. Through the study of hypnotic phenomena, the conception, strange though it was at first, has become familiar, that in one and the same individual several mental groupings are possible, which may remain relatively independent of each other, "know nothing" of each other, and which may cause a splitting of consciousness along lines which they lay down. Cases of such a sort, known as "double personality" ("*double conscience*"), occasionally appear spontaneously. If in such a division of personality consciousness remains constantly bound up with one of the two states, this is called the conscious mental state, and the other the *unconscious*. In the well-known phenomena of so-called post hypnotic suggestion, in which a command given in hypnosis is later executed in the normal state as though by an imperative suggestion, we have an excellent basis for understanding how the unconscious state can influence the conscious, although the latter is ignorant of the existence of the former. In the same way it is quite possible to explain the facts in hysterical cases. Breuer came to the conclusion that the hysterical symptoms originated in such peculiar mental states, which he called "hypnoidal states" (*hypnoide Zustande*). Experiences of an emotional nature, which occur during such hypnoidal states easily become pathogenic, since such states do not present the conditions for a normal draining off of the emotion of the exciting processes. And as a result there arises a peculiar product of this exciting process, that is, the symptom, and this is projected like a foreign body into the normal state. The latter has, then, no conception of the hypnoidal pathogenic situation. Where a symptom arises, we also find an amnesia, a memory gap, and the filling of this gap includes the removal of the conditions under which the symptom originated.

I am afraid that this portion of my treatment will not seem very clear, but you must remember that we are dealing here with new and difficult views, which perhaps could not be made much clearer. This all goes to show that our knowledge in this field is not yet far advanced. Breuer's idea of the hypnoidal states has, moreover, been shown to be superfluous and a hindrance to further investigation, and has been, dropped from present conceptions of psychoanalysis. Later I shall at least suggest what other influences and processes have been disclosed beside that of the hypnoidal states' to which Breuer limited the casual moment.

You have probably also felt, and rightly, that Breuer's investigations gave you only a very incomplete theory and insufficient explanation of the phenomena which we have observed. But complete theories do not fall from Heaven, and you would have had still greater reason to be distrustful, had any one offered you at the beginning of his observations a well-rounded theory, without any gaps; such a theory could only be the child of his speculations and not the fruit of an unprejudiced investigation of the facts.

Second Lecture

Ladies and Gentlemen: At about the same time that Breuer was using the "talking-cure" with his patient, M. Charcot began in Paris, with the hystericals of the Salpetriere, those researches which were to lead to a new understanding of the disease. These results were, however, not yet known in Vienna. But when about ten years later Breuer and I published our preliminary communication on the psychic mechanism of hysterical phenomena, which grew out of the cathartic treatment of Breuer's first patient, we were both of us under the spell of Charcot's investigations. We made the pathogenic experiences of our patients, which acted as psychic traumata, equivalent to those physical traumata whose influence on hysterical paralyses Charcot had determined; and Breuer's hypothesis of hypnoidal states is itself only an echo of the fact that Charcot had artificially reproduced those traumata paralyses in hypnosis.

The great French observer, whose student I was during the years 1885-86, had no natural bent for creating psychological theories. His student, P. Janet, was the first to attempt to penetrate more deeply into the psychic processes of hysteria, and we followed his example, when we made the mental splitting and the dissociation of personality the central points of our theory. Janet propounds a theory of hysteria which draws upon the principal theories of heredity and degeneration which are current in France. According to his view hysteria is a form of degenerative alteration of the nervous system, manifesting itself in a congenital "weakness" of the function of psychic synthesis. The hysterical patient is from the start incapable of correlating and unifying the manifold of his mental processes, and so there arises the tendency to mental dissociation. If you will permit me to use a banal but clear illustration, Janet's hysterical reminds one of a weak woman who has been shopping, and is now on her way home, laden with packages and bundles of every description. She cannot manage the whole lot with her two arms and her ten fingers, and soon she drops one. When she stoops to pick this up, another breaks loose, and so it goes on.

Now it does not agree very well with this assumed mental weakness of hystericals, that there can be observed in hysterical cases, besides the phenomena of lessened functioning, examples of a partial increase of functional capacity, as a sort of compensation. At the time when Breuer's patient had forgotten her mother-tongue and all other languages save English, her control of English attained such a level that if a German book was put before her she could give a fluent, perfect translation of its contents at sight. When later I undertook to continue on my own account the investigations begun by Breuer, I soon came to another view of the origin of hysterical dissociation (or splitting of consciousness). It was inevitable that my views should diverge widely and radically, for my point of departure was not, like that of Janet, laboratory researches, but attempts at therapy. Above everything else, it was practical needs that urged me on. The cathartic treatment, as Breuer had made use of it, presupposed that the patient should be put in deep hypnosis, for only in hypnosis was available the knowledge of his pathogenic associations, which were unknown to him in his normal state. Now hypnosis, as a fanciful, and so to speak, mystical, aid, I soon came to dislike; and when I discovered that, in spite of all my efforts, I could not hypnotize by any means all of my patients, I resolved to give up hypnotism and to make the cathartic method independent of it.

Since I could not alter the psychic state of most of my patients at my wish, I directed my efforts to working with them in their normal state. This seems at first sight to be a particularly senseless and aimless undertaking. The problem was this: to find out something from the patient that the doctor did not know and the patient himself did not know. How could one hope to make such a method succeed? The memory of a very noteworthy and instructive proceeding came to my aid, which I had seen in Bernheim's clinic at Nancy. Bernheim showed us that persons put in a condition of hypnotic somnambulism, and subjected to all sorts of experiences, had only apparently lost the memory of those somnambulic experiences, and that their memory of them could be awakened even in the normal state. If he asked them about their experiences during somnambulism, they said at first that they did not remember, but if he persisted, urged, assured them that they did know, then every time the forgotten memory came back.

Accordingly I did this with my patients. When I had reached in my procedure with them a point at which they declared that they knew nothing more, I would assure them that they did know, that they must just tell it out, and I would venture the assertion that the memory which would emerge at the moment that I laid my hand on the patient's forehead would be the right one. In this way I succeeded, without hypnosis, in learning from the patient all that was necessary for a construction of the connection between the forgotten pathogenic scenes and the symptoms which they had left behind. This was a troublesome and in its length an exhausting proceeding, and did not lend itself to a finished technique. But I did not give it up without drawing definite conclusions from the data which I had gained. I had substantiated the fact that the forgotten memories were not lost. They were in the possession of the patient, ready to emerge and form associations with his other mental content, but hindered from becoming conscious, and forced to remain in the unconscious by some sort of a force. The existence of this force could be assumed with certainty, for in attempting to drag up the unconscious memories into the consciousness of the patient, in opposition to this force, one got the sensation of his own personal effort striving to overcome it. One could get an idea of this force, which maintained the pathological situation, from the resistance of the patient.

It is on this idea of *resistance* that I based my theory of the psychic processes of hystericals. It had been found that in order to cure the patient it was necessary that this force should be overcome. Now with the mechanism of the cure as a starting point, quite a definite theory could be constructed. These same forces, which in the present situation as resistances opposed the emergence of the forgotten ideas into consciousness, must themselves have caused the forgetting, and repressed from consciousness the pathogenic experiences. I called this hypothetical process repression" (*Verdrangung*), and considered that it was proved by the undeniable existence of resistance.

But now the question arose: what were those forces, and what were the conditions of this repression, in which we were now able to recognize the pathogenic mechanism of hysteria? A comparative study of the pathogenic situations, which the cathartic treatment has made possible, allows us to answer this question. In all those experiences, it had happened that a wish had been aroused, which was in sharp opposition to the other desires of the individual, and was not capable of being reconciled with the ethical, aesthetic and personal pretensions of the patient's personality. There had been a short conflict, and the end of this inner struggle was the repression of the idea which presented itself to consciousness as the bearer of this irreconcilable wish. This was, then, repressed from consciousness and forgotten. The incompatibility of the idea in question with the "ego" of the patient was the motive of the repression, the ethical and other pretensions of the individual were the repressing forces. The presence of the incompatible wish, or the duration of the conflict, had given rise to a high degree of mental pain; this pain was avoided by the repression. This latter process is evidently in such a case a device for the protection of the personality.

I will not multiply examples, but will give you the history of a single one of my cases, in which the conditions and the utility of the repression process stand out clearly enough. Of course for my purpose I must abridge the history of the case and omit many valuable theoretical considerations. It is that of a young girl, who was deeply attached to her father, who had died a short time before, and in whose care she had shared -- a situation analogous to that of Breuer's patient.

When her older sister married, the girl grew to feel a peculiar sympathy for her new brother-in-law, which easily passed with her for family tenderness. This sister soon fell ill and died, while the patient and her mother were away. The absent ones were hastily recalled, without being told fully of the painful situation. As the girl stood by the bedside of her dead sister, for one short moment there surged up in her mind an idea, which might be framed in these words: "Now he is free and can marry me." We may be sure that this idea, which betrayed to her consciousness her intense love for her brother-in-law, of which she had not been conscious, was the next moment consigned to repression by her revolted feelings. The girl fell ill with severe hysterical symptoms, and, when I came to treat the case, it appeared that she had entirely forgotten that scene at her sister's bedside and the unnatural, egoistic desire which had arisen in her.

She remembered it during the treatment, reproduced the pathogenic moment with every sign of intense emotional excitement, and was cured by this treatment.

Perhaps I can make the process of repression and its necessary relation to the resistance of the patient, more concrete by a rough illustration, which I will derive from our present situation.

Suppose that here in this hall and in this audience, whose exemplary stillness and attention I cannot sufficiently commend, there is an individual who is creating a disturbance, and, by his ill-bred laughing, talking, by scraping his feet, distracts my attention from my task. I explain that I cannot go on with my lecture under these conditions, and thereupon several strong men among you get up, and, after a short struggle, eject the disturber of the peace from the hall. He is now "repressed," and I can continue my lecture. But in order that the disturbance may not be repeated, in case the man who has just been thrown out attempts to force his way back into the room, the gentlemen who have executed my suggestion take their chairs to the door and establish themselves there as a "resistance," to keep up the repression. Now, if you transfer both locations to the psyche, calling this "consciousness," and the outside the "unconscious," you have a tolerably good illustration of the process of repression.

We can see now the difference between our theory and that of Janet. We do not derive the psychic fission from a congenital lack of capacity on the part of the mental apparatus to synthesize its experiences, but we explain it dynamically by the conflict of opposing mental forces, we recognize in it the result of an active striving of each mental complex against the other.

New questions at once arise in great number from our theory. The situation of psychic conflict is a very frequent one; an attempt of the ego to defend itself from painful memories can be observed everywhere, and yet the result is not a mental fission. We cannot avoid the assumption that still other conditions are necessary, if the conflict is to result in dissociation. I willingly concede that with the assumption of "repression" we stand, not at the end, but at the very beginning of a psychological theory. But we can advance only one step at a time, and the completion of our knowledge must await further and more thorough work.

Now do not attempt to bring the case of Breuer's patient under the point of view of repression. This history cannot be subjected to such an attempt, for it was gained with the help of hypnotic influence. Only when hypnosis is excluded can you see the resistances and repressions and get a correct idea of the pathogenic process. Hypnosis conceals the resistances and so makes a certain part of the mental field freely accessible. By this same process the resistances on the borders of this field are heaped up into a rampart, which makes all beyond inaccessible.

The most valuable things that we have learned from Breuer's observations were his conclusions as to the connection of the symptoms with the pathogenic experiences or psychic traumata, and we must not neglect to evaluate this result properly from the standpoint of the repression-theory. It is not at first evident how we can get from the repression to the creation of the symptoms. Instead of giving a complicated theoretical derivation, I will return at this point to the illustration which I used to typify repression.

Remember that with the ejection of the rowdy and the establishment of the watchers before the door, the affair is not necessarily ended. It may very well happen that the ejected man, now embittered and quite careless of consequences, gives us more to do. He is no longer among us, we are free from his presence, his scornful laugh, his half-audible remarks, but in a certain sense the repression has miscarried, for he makes a terrible uproar outside, and by his outcries and by hammering on the door with his fists interferes with my lecture more than before. Under these circumstances it would be hailed with delight if possibly our honored president, Dr. Stanley Hall, should take upon himself the role of peacemaker and mediator. He would speak with the rowdy on the outside, and then turn to us with recommendation that we let him in again, provided he would guarantee to behave himself better. On Dr. Hall's authority we decide to stop the repression, and now quiet and peace reign again. This is in fact a fairly good presentation of the task devolving upon the physician in the psychoanalytic therapy of neuroses. To say the same thing more directly: we come to the conclusion, from working with hysterical patients and other neurotics, that they have not fully succeeded in repressing the idea to which the incompatible wish is attached. They have, indeed, driven it out of consciousness and out of memory, and apparently saved themselves a great amount of psychic pain, *but in the unconscious the suppressed wish still exists*, only waiting for its chance to become active, and finally succeeds in sending into consciousness, instead of the repressed idea, a disguised and unrecognizable surrogate-creation

(*Ersatzbildung*), to which the same painful sensations associate themselves that the patient thought he was rid of through his repression. This surrogate of the suppressed idea -- the symptom -- is secure against further attacks from the defenses of the ego, and instead of a short conflict there originates now a permanent suffering. We can observe in the symptom, besides the tokens of its disguise, a remnant of traceable similarity with the originally repressed idea; the way in which the surrogate is built up can be discovered during the psychoanalytic treatment of the patient, and for his cure the symptom must be traced back over the same route to the repressed idea. If this repressed material is once more made part of the conscious mental functions -- a process which supposes the overcoming of considerable resistance -- the psychic conflict which then arises, the same which the patient wished to avoid, is made capable of a happier termination, under the guidance of the physician, than is offered by repression. There are several possible suitable decisions which can bring conflict and neurosis to a happy end; in particular cases the attempt may be made to combine several of these. Either the personality of the patient may be convinced that he has been wrong in rejecting the pathogenic wish, and he may be made to accept it either wholly or in part; or this wish may itself be directed to a higher goal which is free from objection, by what is called *sublimation (Sublimierung)*; or the rejection may be recognized as rightly motivated, and the automatic and therefore insufficient mechanism of repression be reinforced by the higher, more characteristically human mental faculties: one succeeds in mastering his wishes by conscious thought.

Forgive me if I have not been able to present more clearly these main points of the treatment which is today known as "psychoanalysis." The difficulties do not lie merely in the newness of the subject.

Regarding the nature of the unacceptable wishes, which succeed in making their influence felt out of the unconscious, in spite of repression; and regarding the question of what subjective and constitutional factors must be present for such a failure of repression and such a surrogate or symptom creation to take place, we will speak in later remarks.

Third Lecture

Ladies and Gentlemen: It is not always easy to tell the truth, especially when one must be brief, and so today I must correct an incorrect statement that I made in my last lecture.

I told you how when I gave up using hypnosis I pressed my patients to tell me what came into their minds that had to do with the problem we were working on.

I told them that they would remember what they had apparently forgotten, and that the thought which irrupted into consciousness (*Einfall*) would surely embody the memory for which we were seeking. I claimed that I substantiated the fact that the first idea of my patients brought the right clew and could be shown to be the forgotten continuation of the memory. Now this is not always so; I represented it as being so simple only for purposes of abbreviation. In fact, it would only happen the first time that the right forgotten material would emerge through simple pressure on my part. If the experience was continued, ideas emerged in every case which could not be the right ones, for they were not to the purpose, and the patients themselves rejected them as incorrect. Pressure was of no further service here, and one could only regret again having given up hypnosis. In this state of perplexity I clung to a prejudice which years later was proved by my friend C. G. Jung of the University of Zurich and his pupils to have a scientific justification. I must confess that it is often of great advantage to have prejudices. I put a high value on the strength of the determination of mental processes, and I could not believe that any idea which occurred to the patient, which originated in a state of concentrated attention, could be quite arbitrary and out of all relation to the forgotten idea that we were seeking. That it was not identical with the latter, could be satisfactorily explained by the hypothetical psychological situation. In the patients whom I treated there were two opposing forces: on the one hand the conscious striving to drag up into consciousness the forgotten experience which was present in the unconscious; and on the other hand the resistance which we have seen, which set itself against the emergence of the suppressed idea or its associates into consciousness. In case this resistance was nonexistent or very slight, the forgotten material could become conscious without disguise (*Enstellung*). It was then a natural supposition that the disguise would be more complete, the greater the resistance to the emergence of the idea. Thoughts which broke into the patient's consciousness instead of the ideas sought for, were accordingly made up just like symptoms; they were new, artificial, ephemeral surrogates for the repressed ideas, and differed from these just in proportion as they had been more completely disguised under the influence of the resistances. These surrogates must, however, show a certain similarity with the ideas which are the object of our search, by virtue of their nature as symptoms; and when the resistance is not too intensive it is possible from the nature of these irruptions to discover the hidden object of our search. This must be related to the repressed thought as a sort of allusion, as a statement of the same thing in *indirect* terms.

We know cases in normal psychology in which analogous situations to the one which we have assumed give rise to similar experiences. Such a case is that of wit. By my study of psychoanalytic technique I was necessarily led to a consideration of the problem of the nature of wit. I will give one example of this sort, which, too, is a story that originally appeared in English.

The anecdote runs: Two unscrupulous business men had succeeded by fortunate speculations in accumulating a large fortune, and then directed their efforts to breaking into good society. Among other means they thought it would be of advantage to be painted by the most famous and expensive artist of the city, a man whose paintings were considered as events. The costly paintings were first shown at a great soiree and both hosts led the most influential connoisseur and art critic to the wall of the salon on which the portraits were hung, to elicit his admiring judgment. The critic looked for a long time, looked about as though in search of something, and then merely asked, pointing out the vacant space between the two pictures: "And where is the Saviour?"

I see that you are all laughing over this good example of wit, which we will now attempt to analyze. We understand that the critic means to say: "You are a couple of malefactors, like those between whom the Saviour was crucified." But he does not say this, he expresses himself instead in a way that at first seems not to the purpose and not related to the matter in hand, but which at the next moment we recognize as an *allusion* to the insult at which he aims, and as a perfect surrogate for it. We cannot expect to find in the case of wit all those relations that our theory supposes for the origin of the irruptive ideas of our patients, but it is my desire to lay stress on the similar motivation of wit and irruptive idea. Why does not the critic say directly what he has to say to the two rogues? Because, in addition to his desire to say it straight out, he is actuated by strong opposite motives. It is a proceeding which is liable to be dangerous to offend people who are one's hosts, and who can call to their aid the strong arms of numerous servants. One might easily suffer the same fate that I used in the previous lecture to illustrate repression. On this ground, the critic does not express the particular insult directly, but in a disguised form, as an allusion with omission. The same constellation comes into play, according to our hypotheses, when our patient produces the irruptive idea as a surrogate for the forgotten idea which is the object of the quest.

Ladies and Gentlemen, it is very useful to designate a group of ideas which belong together and have a common emotive tone, according to the custom of the Zurich school (Bleuler, Jung and others), as a "complex." So we can say that if we set out from the last memories of the patient to look for a repressed complex, we have every prospect of discovering it, if only the patient will communicate to us a sufficient number of the ideas which come into his head. So we let the patient speak along any line that he desires, and cling to the hypothesis that nothing can occur to him except what has some indirect bearing on the complex that we are seeking. If this method of discovering the repressed complexes seems too circumstantial, I can at least assure you that it is the only available one.

In practicing this technique, one is further bothered by the fact that the patient often stops, is at a standstill, and considers that he has nothing to say; nothing occurs to him. If this were really the case and the patient were right, our procedure would again be proven inapplicable. Closer observation shows that such an absence of ideas never really occurs, and that it only appears to when the patient holds back or rejects the idea which he perceives, under the influence of the resistance, which disguises itself as critical judgment of the value of the idea. The patient can be protected from this if he is warned in advance of this circumstance, and told to take no account of the critical attitude. He must say anything that comes into his mind, fully laying aside such critical choice, even though he may think it is unessential, irrelevant, nonsensical, especially when the idea is one which is unpleasant to dwell on. By following this prescription we secure the material which sets us on the track of the repressed complex.

These irruptive ideas, which the patient himself values little, if he is under the influence of the resistance and not that of the physician, are for the psychologist like the ore, which by simple methods of interpretation he reduces from its crude state to valuable metal. If one desires to gain in a short time a preliminary knowledge of the patient's repressed complexes, without going into the question of their arrangement and association experiments, as Jung and his pupils have perfected them. This procedure is to the psychologist what qualitative analysis is to the chemist; it may be dispensed with in the therapy of neurotic patients, but is indispensable in the investigations of the psychoses, which have been begun by the Zurich school with such valuable results.

This method of work with whatever comes into the patient's head when he submits to psychoanalytic treatment, is not the only technical means at our disposal for the widening of consciousness. Two other methods of procedure serve the same purpose, the interpretation of his dreams and the evaluation of acts which he bungles or does without intending to (*Fehl- und Zufallshandlungen*).

I might say, esteemed hearers, that for a long time I hesitated whether instead of this hurried survey of the whole field of psychoanalysis, I should not rather offer you a thorough consideration of the analysis of dreams; a purely subjective and apparently secondary motive decided me against this. It seemed rather an impropriety that in this country, so devoted to practical pursuits, I should pose as "interpreter of dreams," before you had a chance to discover what significance the old and despised art can claim.

Interpretation of dreams is in fact the *via regia* to the interpretation of the unconscious, the surest ground of psychoanalysis and a field in which every worker must win his convictions and gain his education. If I were asked how one could become a psychoanalyst, I should answer, through the study of his own dreams. With great tact all opponents of the psychoanalytic theory have so far either evaded any criticism of the *Traumdeutung* or have attempted to pass over it with the most superficial objections. If, on the contrary, you will undertake the solution of the problems of dream life, the novelties which psychoanalysis present to your thoughts will no longer be difficulties.

You must remember that our nightly dream productions show the greatest outer similarity and inner relationship to the creations of the insane, but on the other hand are compatible with full health during waking life. It does not sound at all absurd to say that whoever regards these normal sense illusions, these delusions and alterations of character as matter for amazement instead of understanding, has not the least prospect of understanding the abnormal creations of diseased mental states in any other than the lay sense. You may with confidence place in this lay group all the psychiatrists of today. Follow me now on a brief excursion through the field of dream problems.

In our waking state we usually treat dreams with as little consideration as the patient treats the irruptive ideas which the psychoanalyst demands from him. It is evident that we reject them, for we forget them quickly and completely. The slight valuation which we place on them is based, with those dreams that are not confused and nonsensical, on the feeling that they are foreign to our personality, and, with other dreams on their evident absurdity and senselessness. Our rejection derives support from the unrestrained shamelessness and the immoral longings which are obvious in many dreams. Antiquity, as we know, did not share this light valuation of dreams. The lower classes of our people today stick close to the value which they set on dreams; they, however, expect from them, as did the ancients, the revelation of the future. I confess that I see no need to adopt mystical hypotheses to fill out the gaps in our present knowledge, and so I have never been able to find anything that supported the hypothesis of the prophetic nature of dreams. Many other things, which are wonderful enough, can be said about them.

And first, not all dreams are so foreign to the character of the dreamer, are incomprehensible and confused. If you will undertake to consider the dreams of young children from the age of a year and a half on, you will find them quite simple and easy to interpret. The young child always dreams of the fulfillment of wishes which were aroused in him the day before and were not satisfied. You need no art of interpretation to discover this simple solution, you only need to inquire into the experiences of the child on the day before (the "dream day"). Now it would certainly be a most satisfactory solution of the dream-riddle, if the dreams of adults, too, were the same as those of children, fulfillments of wishes which had been aroused in them during the dream day. This is actually the fact; the difficulties which stand in the way of this solution can be removed step by step by a thorough analysis of the dream.

There is, first of all, the most weighty objection, that the dreams of adults generally have an incomprehensible content, which shows wishfulfillment least of anything. The answer is this: these dreams have undergone a process of disguise, the psychic content which underlies them was originally meant for quite different verbal expression. You must differentiate between the *manifest dream-content*, which we remember in the morning only confusedly, and with difficulty clothe in words which seem arbitrary, and the *latent dream-thoughts*, whose presence in the unconscious we must assume. This distortion of the dream (*Traumentstellung*) is the same process which has been revealed to you in the investigations of the creations (*symptoms*) of hysterical subjects; it points to the fact that the same opposition of psychic forces has its share in the creation of dreams as in the creation of symptoms.

The manifest dream-content is the disguised surrogate for the unconscious dream thoughts, and this disguising is the work of the defensive forces of the ego, of the resistances. These prevent the repressed wishes from entering consciousness during the waking life, and even in the relaxation of sleep they are still strong enough to force them to hide themselves by a sort of masquerading. The dreamer, then, knows just as little the sense of his dream as the hysterical knows the relation and significance of his symptoms. That there are latent dream-thoughts and that between them and the manifest dream-content there exists the relation just described -- of this you may convince yourselves by the analysis of dreams, a procedure the technique of which is exactly that of psychoanalysis. You must abstract entirely from the apparent connection of the elements in the manifest dream and seek for the irruptive ideas which arise through free association, according to the psychoanalytic laws, from each separate dream element. From this material the latent dream thoughts may be discovered, exactly as one divines the concealed complexes of the patient from the fancies connected with his symptoms and memories. From the latent dream thoughts which you will find in this way, you will see at once how thoroughly justified one is in interpreting the dreams of adults by the same rubrics as those of children. What is now substituted for the manifest dream-content is the real sense of the dream, is always clearly comprehensible, associated with the impressions of the day before, and appears as the fulfilling of an unsatisfied wish. The manifest dream, which we remember after waking, may then be described as a *disguised* fulfillment of *repressed* wishes.

It is also possible by a sort of synthesis to get some insight into the process which has brought about the disguise of the unconscious dream thoughts as the manifest dream-content. We call this process "dream-work" (*Traumarbeit*). This deserves our fullest theoretical interest, since here as nowhere else can we study the unsuspected psychic processes which are existent in the unconscious, or, to express it more exactly, *between* two such separate systems as the conscious and the unconscious. Among these newly discovered psychic processes, two, condensation (*Verdichtung*) and displacement or transvaluation, change of psychic accent (*Verschiebung*), stand out most prominently. Dream work is a special case of the reaction of different mental groupings on each other, and as such is the consequence of psychic fission. In all essential points it seems identical with the work of disguise, which changes the repressed complex in the case of failing repression into symptoms.

You will furthermore discover by the analysis of dreams, most convincingly your own, the unsuspected importance of the role which impressions and experiences from early childhood exert on the development of men. In the dream life the child, as it were, continues his existence in the man, with a retention of all his traits and wishes, including those which he was obliged to allow to fall into disuse in his later years. With irresistible might it will be impressed on you by what processes of development, of repression, sublimation and reaction there arises out of the child, with its peculiar gifts and tendencies, the so-called normal man, the bearer and partly the victim of our painfully acquired civilization. I will also direct your attention to the fact that we have discovered from the analysis of dreams that the unconscious makes use of a sort of symbolism, especially in the presentation of sexual complexes. This symbolism in part varies with the individual, but in part is of a typical nature, and seems to be identical with the symbolism which we suppose to lie behind our myths and legends. It is not impossible that these later creations of the people may find their explanation from the study of dreams.

Finally, I must remind you that you must not be led astray by the objection that the occurrence of anxiety-dreams (*Angsttraume*), contradicts our idea of the dream as a wish-fulfillment. Apart from the consideration that anxiety-dreams also require interpretation before judgment can be passed on them, one can say quite generally that the anxiety does not depend in such a simple way on the dream content as one might suppose without more knowledge of the facts, and more attention to the conditions of neurotic anxiety. Anxiety is one of the ways in which the ego relieves itself of repressed wishes which have become too strong and so is easy to explain in the dream, if the dream has gone too far towards the fulfilling of the objectionable wish.

You see that the investigation of dreams was justified by the conclusions which it has given us concerning things otherwise hard to understand. But we came to it in connection with the psychoanalytic treatment of neurotics. From what has been said you can easily understand how the interpretation of dreams, if it is not made too difficult by the resistance of the patient, can lead to a knowledge of the patient's concealed and repressed wishes and the complexes which he is nourishing. I may now pass to that group of everyday mental phenomena whose study has become a technical help for psychoanalysis.

These are the bungling of acts (*Fehlhandlungen*) among normal men as well as among neurotics, to which no significance is ordinarily attached; the forgetting of things which one is supposed to know and at other times really does know (for example the temporary forgetting of proper names); mistakes in speaking (*Versprechen*), which occur so frequently; analogous mistakes in writing (*Verschreiben*) and in reading (*Verlesen*), the automatic execution of purposive acts in wrong situations (*Vergreifen*) and the loss or breaking of objects, etc. These are trifles, for which no one has ever sought a psychological determination, which have passed unchallenged as chance experiences, as consequences of absent-mindedness, inattention and similar conditions. Here, too, are included the acts and gestures executed without being noticed by the subject, to say nothing of the fact that he attaches no psychic importance to them; as playing and trifling with objects, humming melodies, handling one's person and clothing and the like.

These little things, the bungling of acts, like the symptomatic and chance acts (*Symptom- und Zufallshandlungen*) are not so entirely without meaning as is generally supposed by a sort of tacit agreement. They have a meaning, generally easy and sure to interpret from the situation in which they occur, and it can be demonstrated that they either express impulses and purposes which are repressed, hidden if possible from the consciousness of the individual, or that they spring from exactly the same sort of repressed wishes and complexes which we have learned to know already as the creators of symptoms and dreams.

It follows that they deserve the rank of symptoms, and their observation, like that of dreams, can lead to the discovery of the hidden complexes of the psychic life. With their help one will usually betray the most intimate of his secrets. If these occur so easily and commonly among people in health, with whom repression has on the whole succeeded fairly well, this is due to their insignificance and their inconspicuous nature. But they can lay claim to high theoretic value, for they prove the existence of repression and surrogate creations even under the conditions of health. You have already noticed that the psychoanalyst is distinguished by an especially strong belief in the determination of the psychic life. For him there is in the expressions of the psyche nothing trifling, nothing arbitrary and lawless, he expects everywhere a widespread motivation, where customarily such claims are not made; more than that, he is even prepared to find a manifold motivation of these psychic expressions, while our supposedly inborn causal need is satisfied with a single psychic cause.

Now keeping in mind the means which we possess for the discovery of the hidden, forgotten, repressed things in the soul life: the study of the irruptive ideas called up by free association, the patient's dreams, and his bungled and symptomatic acts; and adding to these the evaluation of other phenomena which emerge during the psychoanalytic treatment, on which I shall later make a few remarks under the heading of "transfer" (*Uebertragung*) you will come with me to the conclusion that our technique is already sufficiently efficacious for the solution of the problem of how to introduce the pathogenic psychic material into consciousness, and so to do away with the suffering brought on by the creation of surrogate symptoms.

The fact that by such therapeutic endeavors our knowledge of the mental life of the normal and the abnormal is widened and deepened, can of course only be regarded as an especial attraction and superiority of this method.

I do not know whether you have gained the impression that the technique through whose arsenal I have led you is a peculiarly difficult one. I consider that on the contrary for one who has mastered it, it is quite adapted for use. But so much is sure, that it is not obvious, that it must be learned no less than the histological or the surgical technique.

You may be surprised to learn that in Europe we have heard very frequently judgments passed on psychoanalysis by persons who knew nothing of its technique and had never practiced it, but who demanded scornfully that we show the correctness of our results. There are among these people some who are not in other things unacquainted with scientific methods of thought, who for example would not reject the result of a microscopical research because it cannot be confirmed with the naked eye in anatomical preparations, and who would not pass judgment until they had used the microscope. But in matters of psychoanalysis circumstances are really more unfavorable for gaining recognition. Psychoanalysis will bring the repressed in mental life to conscious acknowledgement, and everyone who judges it is himself a man who has such repressions, perhaps maintained only with difficulty. It will consequently call forth the same resistances from him as from the patient, and this resistance can easily succeed in disguising itself as intellectual rejection, and bring forward arguments similar to those from which we protect our patients by the basic principles of psychoanalysis. It is not difficult to substantiate in our opponents the same impairment of intelligence produced by emotivity which we may observe every day with our patients. The arrogance of consciousness which for example rejects dreams so lightly, belongs -- quite generally -- to the strongest protective apparatus which guards us against the breaking through of the unconscious complexes, and as a result it is hard to convince people of the reality of the unconscious, and to teach them anew what their conscious knowledge contradicts.

Fourth Lecture

Ladies and Gentlemen: At this point you will be asking what the technique which I have described has taught us of the nature of the pathogenic complexes and repressed wishes of neurotics.

One thing in particular: psychoanalytic investigations trace back the symptoms of disease with really surprising regularity to impressions from the sexual life, show us that the pathogenic wishes are of the nature of erotic impulse-components (*Triebkomponente*), and necessitate the assumption that to disturbances of the erotic sphere must be ascribed the greatest significance among the etiological factors of the disease. This holds of both sexes.

I know that this assertion will not willingly be credited. Even those investigators who gladly follow my psychological labors, are inclined to think that I overestimate the etiological share of the sexual moments. They ask me why other mental excitations should not lead to the phenomena of repression and surrogate-creation which I have described. I can give them this answer; that I do not know why they should not do this, I have no objection to their doing it, but experience shows that they do not possess such a significance, and that they merely support the effect of the sexual moments, without being able to supplant them. This conclusion was not a theoretical postulate; in the *Studien uber Hysterie*, published in 1895 with Dr. Breuer, I did not stand on this ground. I was converted to it when my experience was richer and had led me deeper into the nature of the case. Gentlemen, there are among you some of my closest friends and adherents, who have traveled to Worcester with me. Ask them, and they will tell you that they all were at first completely skeptical of the assertion of the determinative significance of the sexual etiology, until they were compelled by their own analytic labors to come to the same conclusion.

The conduct of the patients does not make it any easier to convince one's self of the correctness of the view which I have expressed. Instead of willingly giving us information concerning their sexual life, they try to conceal it by every means in their power. Men generally are not candid in sexual matters. They do not show their sexuality freely, but they wear a thick overcoat -- a fabric of lies --

to conceal it, as though it were bad weather in the world of sex. And they are not wrong; sun and wind are not favorable in our civilized society to any demonstration of sex life. In truth no one can freely disclose his erotic life to his neighbor. But when your patients see that in your treatment they may disregard the conventional restraints, they lay aside this veil of lies, and then only are you in a position to formulate a judgment of the question in dispute. Unfortunately physicians are not favored above the rest of the children of men in their personal relationship to the questions of the sex life. Many of them are under the ban of that mixture of prudery and lasciviousness which determines the behavior of most *Kulturmenschen* in affairs of sex.

Now to proceed with the communication of our results. It is true that in another series of cases psychoanalysis at first traces the symptoms back not to the sexual, but to banal traumatic experiences. But the distinction loses its significance through other circumstances. The work of analysis which is necessary for the thorough explanation and complete cure of a case of sickness does not stop in any case with the experience of the time of onset of the disease, but in every case it goes back to the adolescence and the early childhood of the patient. Here only do we hit upon the impressions and circumstances which determine the later sickness. Only the childhood experiences can give the explanation for the sensitivity to later traumata and only when these memory traces, which almost always are forgotten, are discovered and made conscious, is the power developed to banish the symptoms. We arrive here at the same conclusion as in the investigation of dreams -- that it is the incompatible, repressed wishes of childhood, which lend their power to the creation of symptoms. Without these the reactions upon later traumata discharge normally. But we must consider these mighty wishes of childhood very generally as sexual in nature.

Now I can at any rate be sure of your astonishment. Is there an infantile sexuality? you will ask. Is childhood not rather that period of life which is distinguished by the lack of the sexual impulse? No, gentlemen, it is not at all true that the sexual impulse enters into the child at puberty, as the devils in the gospel entered into the swine. The child has his sexual impulses and activities from the beginning, he brings them with him into the world, and from these the so-called normal sexuality of adults emerges by a significant development through manifold stages. It is not very difficult to observe the expressions of this childish sexual activity; it needs rather a certain art to overlook them or to fail to interpret them.

As fate would have it, I am in a position to call a witness for my assertions from your own midst. I show you here the work of one, Dr. Sanford Bell, published in 1902 in the *American Journal of Psychology*. The author was a fellow of Clark University, the same institution within whose walls we now stand. In this thesis, entitled A Preliminary Study of the Emotion of Love between the Sexes, which appeared three years before my "Drei Abhandlungen zur

Sexualtheorie," the author says just what I have been saying to you: "The emotion of sex love . . . does not make its appearance for the first time at the period of adolescence as has been thought." He has, as we should say in Europe, worked by the American method, and has gathered not less than 2,500 positive observations in the course of fifteen years, among them 800 of his own. He says of the signs by which this amorous condition manifests itself: "The unprejudiced mind, in observing these manifestations in hundreds of couples of children, cannot escape referring them to sex origin. The most exacting mind is satisfied when to these observations are added the confessions of those who have as children experienced the emotion to a marked degree of intensity, and whose memories of childhood are relatively distinct." Those of you who are unwilling to believe in infantile sexuality will be most astonished to hear that among those children who fell in love so early not a few are of the tender ages of three, four, and five years.

It would not be surprising if you should believe the observations of a fellow-countryman rather than my own. Fortunately a short time ago from the analysis of a five-year-old boy who was suffering from anxiety, an analysis undertaken with correct technique by his own father, I succeeded in getting a fairly complete picture of the bodily expressions of the impulse and the mental productions of an early stage of childish sexual life. And I must remind you that my friend, Dr. C. G. Jung, read you a few hours ago in this room an observation on a still younger girl who from the same cause as my patient—the birth of a little child in the family -- betrayed certainly almost the same secret excitement, wish and complex-creation. Accordingly I am not without hope that you may feel friendly toward this idea of infantile sexuality that was so strange at first. I might also quote the remarkable example of the Zurich psychiatrist, E. Bleuler, who said a few years ago openly that he faced my sexual theories incredulous and bewildered, and since that time by his own observations had substantiated them in their whole scope. If it is true that most men, medical observers and others, do not want to know anything about the sexual life of the child, the fact is capable of explanation only too easily. They have forgotten their own infantile sexual activity under the pressure of education for civilization and do not care to be reminded now of the repressed material. You will be convinced otherwise if you begin the investigation by a self-analysis, by an interpretation of your own childhood memories.

Lay aside your doubts and let us evaluate the infantile sexuality of the earliest years. The sexual impulse of the child manifests itself as a very complex one, it permits of an analysis into many components, which spring from different sources. It is entirely disconnected from the function of reproduction which it is later to serve. It permits the child to gain different sorts of pleasure sensations, which we include, by the analogues and connections which they show, under the term sexual pleasures. The great source of infantile sexual pleasure is the auto-excitation of certain particularly sensitive parts of the body; besides the genitals are included the rectum and the opening of the urinary canal, and also the skin and other sensory surfaces. Since in this first phase of child sexual life the satisfaction is found on the child's own body and has nothing to do with any other object, we call this phase after a word coined by Havelock Ellis, that of "auto-eroticism." The parts of the body significant in giving sexual pleasure we call "erogenous zones." The thumb-sucking (*Ludeln*) or passionate sucking (*Wonnesaugen*) of very young children is a good example of such an auto-erotic satisfaction of an erogenous zone. The first scientific observer of this phenomenon, a specialist in children's diseases in Budapest by the name of Lindner, interpreted these rightly as sexual satisfaction and described exhaustively their transformation into other and higher forms of sexual gratification. Another sexual satisfaction of this time of life is the excitation of the genitals by masturbation, which has such a great significance for later life and, in the case of many individuals, is never fully overcome. Besides this and other auto-erotic manifestations we see very early in the child the impulse-components of *sexual pleasure*, or, as we may say, of the *libido*, which presupposes a second person as its object. These impulses appear in opposed pairs, as active and passive. The most important representatives of this group are the pleasure in inflicting pain (sadism) and its passive exhibition-pleasure (*Schaulust*). From the first of these later pairs splits off the curiosity for knowledge, as from the latter impulse toward artistic and theatrical representation. Other sexual manifestations of the child can already be regarded from the viewpoint of object-choice, in which the second person plays the prominent part. The significance of this was primarily based upon motives of the impulse of self-preservation. The difference between the sexes plays, however, in the child no very great role. One may attribute to every child, without wronging him, a bit of the homosexual disposition.

The sexual life of the child, rich, but dissociated, in which each single impulse goes about the business of arousing pleasure independently of every other, is later correlated and organized in two general directions, so that by the close of puberty the definite sexual character of the individual is practically finally determined. The single impulses subordinate themselves to the overlordship of the genital zone, so that the whole sexual life is taken over into the service of procreation -- and their gratification is now significant only so far as they help to prepare and promote the true sexual act. On the other hand, object-choice prevails over auto-eroticism, so that now in the sexual life all components of the sexual impulse are satisfied in the loved person. But not all the original impulse-components are given a share in the final shaping of the sexual life. Even before the advent of puberty certain impulses have undergone the most energetic repression under the impulse of education, and mental forces like shame, disgust and morality are developed1 which, like sentinels, keep the repressed wishes in subjection. When there comes, in puberty, the high tide of sexual desire it finds dams in this creation of reactions and resistances. These guide the outflow into the so-called normal channels, and make it impossible to revivify the impulses which have undergone repression.

The most important of these repressed impulses are coprophilism, that is, the pleasure in children connected with the excrements; and further, the tendencies attaching themselves to the persons of the primitive object-choice.

Gentlemen, a sentence of general pathology says that every process of development brings with it the germ of pathological dispositions in so far as it may be inhibited, delayed, or incompletely carried out. This holds for the development of the sexual function, with its many complications. It is not smoothly completed in all individuals, and may leave behind either abnormalities or disposition to later diseases by the way of later falling back or *regression*. It may happen that not all the partial impulses subordinate themselves to the rule of the genital zone. Such an impulse which has remained disconnected brings about what we call a perversion, which may replace the normal sexual goal by one of its own. It may happen, as has been said before, that the auto-eroticism is not fully overcome1 as many sorts of disturbances testify. The originally equal value of both sexes as sexual objects may be maintained and an inclination to homosexual activities in adult life result from this, which, under suitable conditions, rises to the level of exclusive homosexuality. This series of disturbances corresponds to the direct inhibition of development of the sexual function, it includes the perversions and the general *infantilism* of the sex life that are not seldom met with.

The disposition to neuroses is to be derived in another way from an injury to the development of the sex life. The neuroses are related to the perversions as the negative to the positive; in them we find the same impulse-components as in perversions, as bearers of the complexes and as creators of the symptoms; but here they work from out the unconscious. They have undergone a repression, but in spite of this they maintain themselves in the unconscious. Psychoanalysis teaches us that overstrong expression of the impulse in very early life leads to a sort of fixation (*Fixirung*), which then offers a weak point in the articulation of the sexual function. If the exercise of the normal sexual function meets with hindrances in later life, this repression, dating from the time of development, is broken through at just that point at which the infantile fixation took place.

You will now perhaps make the objection: But all that is not sexuality." I have used the word in a very much wider sense than you arc accustomed to understand it. This I willingly concede. But it is a question whether you do not rather use the word in much too narrow a sense when you restrict it to the realm of procreation. You sacrifice by that the understanding of perversions; of the connection between perversion, neurosis, and normal sexual life; and have no means of recognizing, in its true significance, the easily observable beginning of the somatic and mental sexual life of the child. But however you decide about the use of the word, remember that the psychoanalyst understands sexuality in that full sense to which he is led by the evaluation of infantile sexuality.

Now we turn again to the sexual development of the child. We still have much to say here, since we have given more attention to the somatic than to the mental expressions of the sexual life. The primitive object-choice of the child, which is derived from his need of help, demands our further interest. It first attaches to all persons to whom he is accustomed, but soon these give way in favor of his parents. The relation of the child to his parents is, as both direct observation of the child and later analytic investigation of adults agree, not at all free from elements of sexual accessory-excitation (*Miterregung*). The child takes both parents, and especially one, as an object of his erotic wishes. Usually he follows in this the stimulus given by his parents, whose tenderness has very clearly the character of a sex manifestation, though inhibited so far as its goal is concerned. As a rule, the father prefers the daughter, the mother the son; the child reacts to this situation, since, as son, he wishes himself in the place of his father, as daughter, in the place of the mother. The feelings awakened in these relations between parents and children, and, as a resultant of them, those among the children in relation to each other, are not only positively of a tender, but negatively of an inimical sort. The complex built up in this way is destined to quick repression, but it still exerts a great and lasting effect from the unconscious. We must express the opinion that this with its ramifications presents the *nuclear complex* of every neurosis, and so we are prepared to meet with it in a not less effectual way in the other fields of mental life. The myth of King Oedipus, who kills his father and wins his mother as a wife is only the slightly altered presentation of the infantile wish, rejected later by the opposing barriers of incest. Shakespeare's tale of Hamlet rests on the same basis of an incest complex, though better concealed. At the time when the child is still ruled by the still unrepressed nuclear complex, there begins a very significant part of his mental activity which serves sexual interest. He begins to investigate the question of where children come from and guesses more than adults imagine of the true relations by deduction from the signs which he sees. Usually his interest in this investigation is awakened by the threat to his welfare through the birth of another child in the family, in whom at first he sees only a rival. Under the influence of the partial impulses which are active in him he arrives at a number of "infantile sexual theories," as that the same male genitals belong to both sexes, that children are conceived by eating and born through the opening of the intestine, and that sexual intercourse is to be regarded as an inimical act, a sort of overpowering.

But just the unfinished nature of his sexual constitution and the gaps in his knowledge brought about by the hidden condition of the feminine sexual canal, cause the infant investigator to discontinue his work as a failure. The facts of this childish investigation itself as well as the infant sex theories created by it are of determinative significance in the building of the child's character, and in the content of his later neuroses.

It is unavoidable and quite normal that the child should make his parents the objects of his first object-choice. But his libido must not remain fixed on these first chosen objects, but must take them merely as a prototype and transfer from these to other persons in the time of definite object-choice. The breaking loose (*Ablo-sung*) of the child from his parents is thus a problem impossible to escape if the social virtue of the young individual is not to be impaired. During the time that the repressive activity is making its choice among the partial sexual impulses and later, when the influence of the parents, which in the most essential way has furnished the material for these repressions, is lessened, great problems fall to the work of education, which at present certainly does not always solve them in the most intelligent and economic way.

Gentlemen, do not think that with these explanations of the sexual life and the sexual development of the child we have too far departed from psychoanalysis and the cure of neurotic disturbances. If you like, you may regard the psychoanalytic treatment only as a continued education for the overcoming of childhood-remnants (*Kindheitsresten*).

Fifth Lecture

Ladies and Gentlemen: With the discovery of infantile sexuality and the tracing back of the neurotic symptoms to erotic impulse-components we have arrived at several unexpected formulae for expressing the nature and tendencies of neurotic diseases. We see that the individual falls ill when in consequence of outer hindrances or inner lack of adaptability the satisfaction of the erotic needs in the sphere of reality is denied. We see that he then flees to sickness, in order to find with its help a surrogate satisfaction for that denied him. We recognize that the symptoms of illness contain fractions of the sexual activity of the individual, or his whole sexual life, and we find in the turning away from reality the chief tendency and also the chief injury of the sickness. We may guess that the resistance of our patients against the cure is not a simple one, but is composed of many motives. Not only does the ego of the patient strive against the giving up of the repression by which it has changed itself from its original constitution into its present form, but also the sexual impulses may not renounce their surrogate satisfaction so long as it is not certain that they can be offered anything better in the sphere of reality.

The flight from the unsatisfying reality into what we call, on account of its biologically injurious nature, disease, but which is never without an individual gain in pleasure for the patient, takes place over the path of regression, the return to earlier phases of the sexual life, when satisfaction was not lacking. This regression is seemingly a twofold one, a *temporal*, in so far as the *libido* or erotic need falls back to a temporally earlier stage of development, and a *formal*, since the original and primitive psychic means of expression are applied to the expression of this need. Both sorts of regression focus in childhood and have their common point in the production of an infantile condition of sexual life.

The deeper you penetrate into the pathogenic of neurotic diseases, the more the connection of neuroses with other products of human mentality, even the most valuable, will be revealed to you. You will be reminded that we men, with the high claims of our civilization and under the pressure of our repressions, find reality generally quite unsatisfactory and so keep up a life of fancy in which we love to compensate for what is lacking in the sphere of reality by the production of wish-fulfillments. In these phantasies is often contained very much of the particular constitutional essence of personality and of its tendencies, repressed in real life. The energetic and successful man is he who succeeds by dint of labor in transforming his wish fancies into reality. Where this is not successful in consequence of the resistance of the outer world and the weakness of the individual, there begins the turning away from reality. The individual takes refuge in his satisfying world of fancy. Under certain conditions it still remains possible for him to find another connecting link between these fancies and reality, instead of permanently becoming a stranger to it through the regression into the infantile. If the individual who is displeased with reality is in possession of that *artistic talent* which is still a psychological riddle, he can transform his fancies into artistic creations. So he escapes the fate of a neurosis and wins back his connection with reality by this round-about way. Where this opposition to the real world exists, but this valuable talent fails or proves insufficient, it is unavoidable that the *libido*, following the origin of the fancies, succeeds by means of regression in revivifying the infantile wishes and so producing a neurosis. The neurosis takes, in our time, the place of the cloister, in which were accustomed to take refuge all those whom life had undeceived or who felt themselves too weak for life. Let me give at this point the main result at which we have arrived by the psychoanalytic investigation of neurotics, namely, that neuroses have no peculiar psychic content of their own, which is not also to be found in healthy states; or, as C. G. Jung has expressed it, neurotics fall ill of the same complexes with which we sound people struggle. It depends on quantitative relationships, on the relations of the forces wrestling with each other, whether the struggle leads to health, to a neurosis, or to compensatory over-functioning (*Ueberleistung*).

Ladies and Gentlemen, I have still withheld from you the most remarkable experience which corroborates our assumptions of the sexual impulse-forces of neurotics. Every time that we treat a neurotic psychoanalytically, there occurs in him the so-called phenomenon of *transfer* (*Uebertragung*), that is, he applies to the person of the physician a great amount of tender emotion, often mixed with enmity, which has no foundation in any real relation, and must be derived in every respect from the old wish-fancies of the patient which have become unconscious. Every fragment of his emotive life, which can no longer be called back into memory, is accordingly lived over by the patient in his relations to the physician, and only by such a living of them over in the "transfer" is he convinced of the existence and the power of these unconscious sexual excitations. The symptoms, which, to use a simile from chemistry, are the precipitates of earlier love experiences (in the widest sense), can only be dissolved in the higher temperature of the experience of transfer and transformed into other psychic products. The physician plays in this reaction, to use an excellent expression of S. Ferenczi, the role of a *catalytic ferment*, which temporarily attracts to itself the affect which has become free in the course of the process.

The study of transfer can also give you the key to the understanding of hypnotic suggestion, which we at first used with our patients as a technical means of investigation of the unconscious. Hypnosis showed itself at that time to be a therapeutic help, but a hindrance to the scientific knowledge of the real nature of the case, since it cleared away the psychic resistances from a certain field, only to pile them up in an unscalable wall at the boundaries of this field. You must not think that the phenomenon of transfer, about which I can unfortunately say only too little here, is created by the influence of the psychoanalytic treatment. The transfer arises spontaneously in all human relations and in the relations of the patient to the physician; it is everywhere the especial bearer of therapeutic influences, and it works the stronger the less one knows of its presence. Accordingly psychoanalysis does not create it, it merely discloses it to consciousness, and avails itself of it, in order to direct the psychic processes to the wished-for goal. But I cannot leave the theme of transfer without stressing the fact that this phenomenon is of decisive importance to convince not only the patient, but also the physician. I know that all my adherents were first convinced of the correctness of my views through their experience with transfer, and I can very well conceive that one may not win such a surety of judgment so long as he makes no psychoanalysis, and so has not himself observed the effects of transfer.

Ladies and Gentlemen, I am of the opinion that there are, on the intellectual side, two hindrances to acknowledging the value of the psychoanalytic viewpoint: first, the fact that we are not accustomed to reckon with a strict determination of mental life, which holds without exception, and, second, the lack of knowledge of the peculiarities through which unconscious mental processes differ from these conscious ones with which we are familiar. One of the most widespread resistances against the work of psychoanalysis with patients as with persons in health reduces to the latter of the two moments. One is afraid of doing harm by psychoanalysis, one is anxious about calling up into consciousness the repressed sexual impulses of the patient, as though there were danger that they could overpower the higher ethical strivings and rob him of his cultural acquisitions. One can see that the patient has sore places in his soul life, but one is afraid to touch them, lest his suffering be increased. We may use this analogy. It is, of course, better not to touch diseased places when one can only cause pain. But we know that the surgeon does not refrain from the investigation and reinvestigation of the seat of illness, if his invasion has as its aim the restoration of lasting health. Nobody thinks of blaming him for the unavoidable difficulties of the investigation or the phenomena of reaction from the operation, if these only accomplish their purpose, and gain for the patient a final cure by temporarily making his condition worse. The case is similar in psychoanalysis; it can lay claim to the same things as surgery; the increase of pain which takes place in the patient during the treatment is very much less than that which the surgeon imposes upon him, and especially negligible in comparison with the pains of serious illness. But the consequence which is feared, that of a disturbance of the cultural character by the impulse which has been freed from repression, is wholly impossible. In relation to this anxiety we must consider what our experiences have taught us with certainty, that the somatic and mental power of a wish, if once its repression has not succeeded, is incomparably stronger when it is unconscious than when it is conscious, so that by being made conscious it can only be weakened. The unconscious wish cannot be influenced, is free from all strivings in the contrary direction, while the conscious is inhibited by those wishes which are also conscious and which strive against it. The work of psychoanalysis accordingly presents a better substitute, in the service of the highest and most valuable cultural strivings, for the repression which has failed.

Now what is the fate of the wishes which have become free by psychoanalysis, by what means shall they be made harmless for the life of the individual? There are several ways. The general consequence is, that the wish is consumed during the work by the correct mental activity of those better tendencies which are opposed to it. The repression is supplanted by a condemnation carried through with the best means at one's disposal. This is possible, since for the most part we have to abolish only the effects of earlier development stages of the ego. The individual for his part only repressed the useless impulse, because at that time he was himself still incompletely organized and weak; in his present maturity and strength he can, perhaps, conquer without injury to himself that which is inimical to him. A second issue of the work of psychoanalysis may be that the revealed unconscious impulses can now arrive at those useful applications which, in the case of undisturbed developments, they would have found earlier. The extirpation of the infanitle wishes is not at all the ideal aim of development. The neurotic has lost, by his repressions, many sources of mental energy whose contingents would have been very valuable for his character building and his life activities. We know a far more purposive process of development, to so-called sublimation (Sublimirung), by which the energy of infantile wish-excitations is not secluded, but remains capable of application, while for the particular excitations, instead of becoming useless, a higher, eventually no longer sexual, goal is set up The components of the sexual instinct are especially distinguished by such a capacity for the sublimation and exchange of their sexual goal for one more remote and socially more valuable. To the contributions of the energy won in such a way for the functions of our mental life we probably owe the highest cultural consequences. A repression taking place at an early period excludes the sublimation of the repressed impulse; after the removal of the repression the way to sublimation is again free.

We must not neglect, also, to glance at the third of the possible issues. A certain part of the suppressed libidinous excitation has a right to direct satisfaction and ought to find it in life. The claims of our civilization make life too hard for the greater part of humanity, and so further the aversion to reality and the origin of neuroses, without producing an excess of cultural gain by this excess of sexual repression. We ought not to go so far as to fully neglect the original animal part of our nature. We ought not to forget that the happiness of individuals cannot be dispensed with as one of the aims of our culture. The plasticity of the sexual-components, manifest in their capacity for sublimation, may cause a great temptation to accomplish greater culture-effects by a more and more far reaching sublimation. But just as little as with our machines we expect to change more than a certain fraction of the applied heat into useful mechanical work, just as little ought we to strive to separate the sexual impulse in its whole extent of energy from its peculiar goal. This cannot succeed, and if the narrowing of sexuality is pushed too far it will have all the evil effects of a robbery.

I do not know whether you will regard the exhortation with which I close as a presumptuous one. I only venture the indirect presentation of my conviction, if I relate an old tale, whose application you may make yourselves. German literature knows a town called Schilda, to whose inhabitants were attributed all sorts of clever pranks. The wiseacres, so the story goes, had a horse, with whose powers of work they were well satisfied, and against whom they had only one grudge, that he consumed so much expensive oats. They concluded that by good management they would break him of this bad habit, by cutting down his rations by several stalks each day, until he had learned to do without them altogether. Things went finely for a while, the horse was weaned to one stalk a day, and on the next day he would at last work without fodder. On the morning of this day the malicious horse was found dead; the citizens of Schilda could not understand why he had died. We should be inclined to believe that the horse had starved, and that without a certain ration of oats no work could be expected from an animal.

MYSTICISM AND LOGIC

METAPHYSICS, or the attempt to conceive the world as a whole means of thought, has been developed, from the first, by the union and conflict of two very different human impulses, the one urging men towards mysticism, the other urging them towards science. Some men have achieved greatness through one of these impulses alone, others through the other alone: in Hume, for example, the scientific impulse reigns quite unchecked, while in Blake a strong hostility to science coexists with profound mystic insight. But the greatest men who have been philosophers have the felt need both of science and of mysticism: the attempt to harmonize the two was what made their life, and what always must, for all its arduous uncertainty, make philosophy, to some minds, a greater thing than either science or religion.

Before attempting an explicit characterization of the scientific and the mystical impulses, I will illustrate them by examples from two philosophers whose greatness lies in the very intimate blending which they achieved. The two philosophers I mean are Heraclitus and Plato.

Heraclitus, as every one knows, was a believer in universal flux: builds and destroys all things. From the few fragments that remain, it is not easy to discover how he arrived at his opinions, there are some sayings that strongly suggest scientific observation as the source.

'The things that can be seen, heard, and learned,' he says, 'are what I prize the most.' This is the language of the empiricist, to whom observation is the sole guarantee of truth. 'The sun is new every day,' is another fragment; and this opinion, in spite of its paradoxical character, is obviously inspired by scientific reflection, no doubt seemed to him to obviate the difficulty of understanding how the sun can work its way underground from west to east during the night. Actual observation must also have suggested to him his central doctrine, that Fire is the one permanent substance, of which all visible things are passing phases. In combustion we see things change utterly, while their flame and heat rise up into the air and vanish.

'This world, which is the same for all,' he says, 'no one of gods or men has made; but it was ever, is now, and ever shall be, an ever-living Fire, with measures kindling, and measures going out.'

'The transformations of Fire are, first of all, sea; and half of the sea is earth, half whirlwind.'

This theory, though no longer one which science can accept, is nevertheless scientific in spirit. Science, too, might have inspired the famous saying to which Plato alludes: 'You cannot step twice into the same rivers; for fresh waters are ever flowing in upon you.' But we find also another statement among the extant fragments: 'We step and do not step into the same rivers; we are and are not'.

The comparison of this statement, which is mystical, with the one quoted by Plato, which is scientific, shows how intimately the two tendencies are blended in the system of Heraclitus. Mysticism is, in essence, little more than a certain intensity and depth of feeling in regard to what is believed about the universe; and this kind of feeling leads Heraclitus, on the basis of his science, to strangely poignant sayings concerning life and the world, such as:

'Time is a child playing draughts, the kingly power is a child's.'

It is poetic imagination, not science, which presents Time as despotic lord of the world, with all the irresponsible frivolity of a child. It is mysticism, too, which leads Heraclitus to assert the identity of opposites: 'Good and ill are one,' he says; and again: 'To God all things are fair and good and right, but men hold some things wrong and some right.'

Much of mysticism underlies the ethics of Heraclitus. It is true that a scientific determinism alone might have inspired the statement: 'Man's character is his fate;' but only a mystic would have said:

'Every beast is driven to the pasture with blows;' and again:

'It is hard to fight with one's heart's desire. Whatever it wishes to get, it purchases at the cost of soul;' and again:

'Wisdom is one thing. It is to know the thought by which all things are steered through all things.'[1]

Examples might be multiplied, but those that have been given are enough to show the character of the man: the facts of science, as, they appeared to him, fed the flame in his soul, and in its light he saw into the depths of the world by the reflection of his own dancing swiftly penetrating fire. In such a nature we see the true union of the mystic and the man of science -- the highest eminence, as I think, that it is possible to achieve in the world of thought.

---

[1] All the above quotations are from Burnet's *Early Greek Philosophy* (2nd ed.,1908), pp.146-156.

In Plato, the same twofold impulse exists, though the mystic impulse is distinctly the stronger of the two, and secures ultimate victory whenever the conflict is sharp. His description of the cave is the classical statement of belief in a knowledge and reality truer and more real than that of the senses:

'Imagine[2] a number of men living in an underground cavernous chamber, with an entrance open to the light, extending along the entire length of the cavern, in which they have been confined, from their childhood, with their legs and necks so shackled that they are obliged to sit still and look straight forwards, because their chains render it impossible for them to turn their heads round: and imagine a bright fire burning some way off, above and behind them, and an elevated roadway passing between the fire and the prisoners, with a low wall built along it, like the screens which conjurors put up in front of their audience, and above which they exhibit their wonders.

I have it, he replied.

Also figure to yourself a number of persons walking behind this wall, and carrying with them statues of men, and images of other animals, wrought in wood and stone and all kinds of materials, together with various other articles, which overtop the wall; and, as you might expect, let some of the passers-by be talking, and others silent.

You are describing a strange scene, and strange prisoners.

They resemble us, I replied.

Now consider what would happen if the course of nature brought them a release from their letters, and a remedy for their foolishness, in the following manner. Let us suppose that one of them has been released, and compelled suddenly to stand up, and turn his neck round and walk with open eyes towards the light; and let us suppose that he goes through all these actions with pain, and that the dazzling splendour renders him incapable of discerning those objects of which he used formerly to see the shadows. What answer should you expect him to make, if some one were to tell him that in those days he was watching foolish phantoms, but that now he is somewhat nearer to reality, and is turned towards things more real, and sees more correctly; above all, if he were to point out to him the several objects that are passing by, and question him, and compel him to answer what they are? Should you not expect him to be puzzled, and to regard his old visions as truer than the objects now forced upon his notice?

Yes, much truer. . . .

---

[2] *Republic, 514* translated by Davies and Vaughan.

Hence, I suppose, habit will be necessary to enable him to perceive objects in that upper world. At first he will be most successful in distinguishing shadows; then he will discern the reflections of men and other things in water, and afterwards the realities; and after this he will raise his eyes to encounter the light of the moon and stars, finding it less difficult to study the heavenly bodies and the heaven itself by night, than the sun and the sun's light by day.

Doubtless.

Last of all, I imagine, he will be able to observe and contemplate the nature of the sun, not as it *appears* in water or on alien ground, but as it is in itself in its own territory.

Of course.

His next step will be to draw the conclusion, that the sun is the author of the seasons and the years, and the guardian of all things in the visible world, and in a manner the cause of all those things which he and his companions used to see.

Obviously, this will be his next step. . . .

Now this imaginary case, my dear Glaucon, you must apply in all its parts to our former statements, by comparing the region which the eye reveals, to the prison house, and the light of the fire therein to the power of the sun: and if, by the upward ascent and the contemplation of the upper world, you understand the mounting of the soul into the intellectual region, you will hit the tendency of my own surmises, since you desire to be told what they are; though, indeed, God only knows whether they are correct. But, be that as it may, the view which I take of the subject is to the following effect. In the world of knowledge, the essential Form of Good is the limit of our enquiries, and can barely be perceived; but, when perceived, we cannot help concluding that it is in every case the source of all that is bright and beautiful, -- in the visible world giving birth to light and its master, and in the intellectual world dispensing, immediately and with full authority, truth and reason; -- and that whosoever would act wisely, either in private or in public, must set this Form of Good before his eyes.'

But in this passage, as throughout most of Plato's teaching, there is an identification of the good with the truly real, which became embodied in the philosophical tradition, and is still largely operative in our own day. In thus allowing a legislative function to the good, Plato produced a divorce between philosophy and science, from which, in my opinion, both have suffered ever since and are still suffering. The man of science, whatever his hopes may be, must lay them aside while he studies nature; and the philosopher, if he is to achieve truth must do the same. Ethical considerations can only legitimately appear when the truth has been ascertained: they can and should appear as determining our feeling towards the truth, and our manner of ordering our lives in view of the truth, but not as themselves dictating what the truth is to be.

There are passages in Plato -- among those which illustrate the scientific side of his mind -- where he seems clearly aware of this. The most noteworthy is the one in which Socrates, as a young man, is explaining the theory of ideas to Parmenides.

After Socrates has explained that there is an idea of the good, but not of such things as hair and mud and dirt, Parmenides advises him 'not to despise even the meanest things', and this advice shows the genuine scientific temper. It is with this impartial temper that the mystic's apparent insight into a higher reality and a hidden good has to be combined if philosophy is to realise its greatest possibilities. And it is failure in this respect that has made so much of idealistic philosophy thin, lifeless, and insubstantial. It is only in marriage with the world that our ideals can bear fruit: divorced from it, they remain barren. But marriage with the world is not to be achieved by an ideal which shrinks from fact, or demands in advance that the world shall conform to its desires.

Parmenides himself is the source of a peculiarly interesting strain of mysticism which pervades Plato's thought -- the mysticism which may be called 'logical' because it is embodied in theories on logic. This form of mysticism, which appears, so far as the West is concerned, to have originated with Parmenides, dominates the reasonings of all the great mystical metaphysicians from his day to that of Hegel and his modern disciples. Reality, he says, is uncreated, indestructible, unchanging, indivisible; it is 'immovable in the bonds of mighty chains, without beginning and without end; since corning into being and passing away have been driven afar, and true belief has cast them away'. The fundamental principle of his inquiry is stated in a sentence which would not be out of place in Hegel: 'Thou canst not know what is not -- that is impossible -- nor utter it; for it is the same thing that can be thought and that can be.' And again: 'It needs must be that what can be thought and spoken of is; for it is possible for it to be, and it is not possible for what is nothing to be.' The impossibility of change follows from this principle; for what is past can be spoken of, and therefore, by the principle, still is.

Mystical philosophy, in all ages and in all parts of the world, is characterized by certain beliefs which are illustrated by the doctrines we have been considering.

There is, first, the belief in insight as against discursive analytic knowledge: the belief in a way of wisdom, sudden, penetrating, coercive, which is contrasted with the slow and fallible study of outward appearance by a science relying wholly upon the senses. All who are capable of absorption in an inward passion must have experienced at times the strange feeling of unreality in common objects, the loss of contact with daily things, in which the solidity of the outer world is lost, and the soul seems, in utter loneliness, to bring forth, out of its own depths, the mad dance of fantastic phantoms which have hitherto appeared as independently real and living. This is the negative side of the mystic's initiation: the doubt concerning common knowledge, preparing the way for the reception of what seems a higher wisdom. Many men to whom this negative experience is familiar do not pass beyond it, but for the mystic it is merely the gateway to an ampler world.

The mystic insight begins with the sense of a mystery unveiled, of a hidden wisdom now suddenly become certain beyond the possibility of a doubt. The sense of certainty and revelation comes earlier than any definite belief. The definite beliefs at which mystics arrive are the result of reflection upon the inarticulate experience gained in the moment of insight. Often, beliefs which have no real connection with this moment become subsequently attracted into the central nucleus; thus in addition to the convictions which all mystics share, we find, in many of them, other convictions of a more local and temporary character, which no doubt become amalgamated with what was essentially mystical in virtue of their subjective certainty. We may ignore such inessential accretions, and confine ourselves to the beliefs which all mystics share.

The first and most direct outcome of the moment of illumination is belief in the possibility of a way of knowledge which may be called revelation or insight or intuition, as contrasted with sense, reason, and analysis, which are regarded as blind guides leading to the morass of illusion. Closely connected with this belief is the conception of a Reality behind the world of appearance and utterly different from it. This Reality is regarded with an admiration often amounting to worship; it is felt to be always and everywhere close at hand, thinly veiled by the shows of sense, ready, for the receptive mind, to shine in its glory even through the apparent folly and wickedness of Man. The poet, the artist, and the lover are seekers after that glory: the haunting beauty that they pursue is the faint reflection of its sun. But the mystic lives in the full light of the vision: what others dimly seek he knows, with a knowledge beside which all other knowledge is ignorance.

The second characteristic of mysticism is its belief in unity, and its refusal to admit opposition or division anywhere. We found Heraclitus saying 'good and ill are one'; and again he says, 'the way up and the way down is one and the same'. The same attitude appears in the simultaneous assertion of contradictory propositions, such as: 'We step and do not step into the same rivers; we are and are not.' The assertion of Parmenides, that reality is one and indivisible, comes from the same impulse towards unity. In Plato, this impulse is less prominent, being held in check by his theory of ideas; but it reappears, so far as his logic permits, in the doctrine of the primacy of the Good.

A third mark of almost all mystical metaphysics is the denial of the reality of Time. This is an outcome of the denial of division; if all is one, the distinction of past and future must be illusory. We have seen this doctrine prominent in Parmenides; and among moderns it is fundamental in the systems of Spinoza and Hegel.

The last of the doctrines of mysticism which we have to consider is its belief that all evil is mere appearance, an illusion produced by the divisions and oppositions of the analytic intellect. Mysticism does not maintain that such things as cruelty, for example, are good, but it denies that they are real: they belong to that lower world of phantoms from which we are to be liberated by the insight of the vision. Sometimes -- for example in Hegel, and at least verbally in Spinoza -- not only evil, but good also, is regarded as illusory, though nevertheless the emotional attitude towards what is held to be Reality is such as would naturally be associated with the belief that Reality is good. What is, in all cases, ethically characteristic of mysticism is absence of indignation or protest, acceptance with joy, disbelief in the ultimate truth of the division into two hostile camps, the good and the bad. This attitude is a direct outcome of the nature of the mystical experience: with its sense of unity is associated a feeling of infinite peace. Indeed it may be suspected that the feeling of peace produces, as feelings do in dreams, the whole system of associated beliefs which make up the body of mystic doctrine. But this is a difficult question, and one on which it cannot be hoped that mankind will reach agreement.

Four questions thus arise in considering the truth or falsehood of mysticism, namely:

I. Are there two ways of knowing, which may be called respectively reason and intuition? And if so, is either to be preferred to the other?

II. Is all plurality and division illusory?

III. Is time unreal?

IV. What kind of reality belongs to good and evil?

On all four of these questions, while fully developed mysticism seems to me mistaken, I yet believe that, by sufficient restraint, there is an element of wisdom to be learned from the mystical way of feeling, which does not seem to be attainable in any other manner. If this is the truth, mysticism is to be commended as an attitude towards life, not as a creed about the world. The metaphysical creed, I shall maintain, is a mistaken outcome of the emotion, although this emotion, as colouring and informing all other thoughts and feelings, is the inspirer of whatever is best in Man. Even the cautious and patient investigation of truth by science, which seems the very antithesis of the mystic's swift certainty, may be fostered and nourished by that very spirit of reverence in which mysticism lives and moves.

I. REASON AND INTUITION[3]

Of the reality or unreality of the mystic's world I know nothing. I have no wish to deny it, nor even to declare that the insight which reveals it is not a genuine insight. What I do wish to maintain -- and it is here that the scientific attitude becomes imperative -- is that insight, untested and unsupported, is an insufficient guarantee of truth, in spite of the fact that much of the most important truth is first suggested by its means. It is common to speak of an opposition between instinct and reason; in the eighteenth century, the opposition was drawn in favour of reason, but under the influence of Rousseau and the romantic movement instinct was given the preference, first by those who rebelled against artificial forms of government and thought, and then, as the purely rationalistic defence of traditional theology became increasingly difficult, by all who felt in science a menace to creeds which they associated with a spiritual outlook on life and the world. Bergson, under the name of 'intuition', has raised instinct to the position of sole arbiter of metaphysical truth. But in fact the opposition of instinct and reason is mainly illusory. Instinct, intuition or insight is what first leads to the beliefs which subsequent reason confirms or confutes; but the confirmation, where it is possible, consists, in the last analysis, of agreement with other beliefs no less instinctive. Reason is a harmonizing, controlling force rather than a creative one. Even in the most purely logical realm, it is insight that first arrives at what is new.

Where instinct and reason do sometimes conflict is in regard to single beliefs, held instinctively, and held with such determination that no degree of inconsistency with other beliefs leads to their abandonment. Instinct, like all human faculties, is liable to error. Those in whom reason is weak are often unwilling to admit this as regards themselves, though all admit it in regard to others. Where instinct is least liable to error is in practical matters as to which right judgment is a help to survival: friendship and hostility in others, for instance, are often felt with extraordinary discrimination through very careful disguises. But even in such matters a wrong impression may be given by reserve or flattery; and in matters less directly practical, such as philosophy deals with, very strong instinctive beliefs are sometimes wholly mistaken, as we may come to know

---

[3] This section, and also one or two pages in later sections, have been printed in a course of Lowell lectures *On our knowledge of the external world*, published by the Open Court Publishing Company -- But I have left them here, as this is the context for which they were originally written.

through their perceived inconsistency with other equally strong beliefs. It is such considerations that necessitate the harmonizing mediation of reason, which tests our beliefs by their mutual compatibility, and examines, in doubtful cases, the possible sources of error on the one side and on the other. In this there is no opposition to instinct as a whole, but only to blind reliance upon some one interesting aspect of instinct to the exclusion of other more commonplace but not less trustworthy aspects. It is such one-sidedness, not instinct itself, that reason aims at correcting.

These more or less trite maxims may be illustrated by application to Bergson's advocacy of 'intuition' as against 'intellect'. There are, he says, 'two profoundly different ways of knowing a thing. The first implies that we move round the object: the second that we enter into it. The first depends on the point of view at which we are placed and on the symbols by which we express ourselves. The second neither depends on a point of view nor relies on any symbol. The first kind of knowledge may be said to stop at the *relative*; the second, in those cases where it is possible, to attain the *absolute*.'[4] The second of these, which is intuition, is, he says, 'the kind of *intellectual sympathy* by which one places oneself within an object in order to coincide with what is unique in it and therefore inexpressible'. In illustration, he mentions self-knowledge: 'there is one reality, at least, which we all seize from within, by intuition and not by simple analysis. It is our own personality in its flowing through time -- our self which endures'. The rest of Bergson's philosophy consists in reporting, through the imperfect medium of words, the knowledge gained by intuition, and the consequent complete condemnation of all the pretended knowledge derived from science and common sense.

This procedure, since it takes sides in a conflict of instinctive beliefs, stands in need of justification by proving the greater trustworthiness of the beliefs on one side than of those on the other. Bergson attempts this justification in two ways, first by explaining that intellect is a purely practical faculty to secure biological success, secondly by mentioning remarkable feats of instinct in animals and by pointing out characteristics of the world which, though intuition can apprehend them, are baffling to intellect as he interprets it.

Of Bergson's theory that intellect is a purely practical faculty, developed in the struggle for survival, and not a source of true beliefs, we may say, first, that it is only through intellect that we know of the struggle for survival and of the biological ancestry of man: if the intellect is misleading, the whole of this merely inferred history is presumably untrue. If, on the other hand, we agree with him in thinking that evolution took place as Darwin believed, then it is not only intellect,

---

[4]   *Introduction go Metaphysics*, p. l.

but all our faculties, that have been developed under the stress of practical utility. Intuition is seen at its best where it is directly useful, for example in regard to other people's characters and dispositions. Bergson apparently holds that capacity for this kind of knowledge is less explicable by the struggle for existence than, for example, capacity for pure mathematics. Yet the savage deceived by false friendship is likely to pay for his mistake with his life; whereas even in the most civilized societies men are not put to death for mathematical incompetence. All the most striking of his instances of intuition in animals have a very direct survival value. The fact is, of course, that both intuition and intellect have been developed because they are useful, and that, speaking broadly, they are useful when they give truth and become harmful when they give falsehood. Intellect, in civilized man, like artistic capacity, has occasionally been developed beyond the point where it is useful to the individual; intuition, on the other hand, seems on the whole to diminish as civilization increases. It is greater, as a rule, in children than in adults, in the uneducated than in the educated. Probably in dogs it exceeds anything to be found in human beings. But those who see in these facts a recommendation of intuition ought to return to running wild in the woods, dyeing themselves with woad and living on hips and haws.

Let us next examine whether intuition possesses any such infallibility as Bergson claims for it. The best instance of it, according to him, is our acquaintance with ourselves; yet self-knowledge is proverbially rare and difficult. Most men, for example, have in their nature meannesses, vanities and envies of which they are quite unconscious, though even their best friends can perceive them without any difficulty. It is true that intuition has a convincingness which is lacking to intellect: while it is present, it is almost impossible to doubt its truth. But if it should appear, on examination, to be at least as fallible as intellect, its greater subjective certainty becomes a demerit, making it only the more irresistibly deceptive. Apart from self-knowledge, one of the most notable examples of intuition is the knowledge people believe themselves to possess of those with whom they are in love: the wall between different personalities seems to become transparent, and people think they see into another soul as into their own. Yet deception in such cases is constantly practised with success; and even where there is no intentional deception, experience gradually proves, as a rule, that the supposed insight was illusory, and that the slower more groping methods of the intellect are in the long run more reliable.

Bergson maintains that intellect can only deal with things in so far as they resemble what has been experienced in the past, while intuition has the power of apprehending the uniqueness and novelty that always belong to each fresh moment. That there is something unique and new at every moment, is certainly true; it is also true that this cannot be fully expressed by means of intellectual concepts. Only direct acquaintance can give knowledge of what is unique and new. But direct acquaintance of this kind is given fully in sensation, and does not require, so far as I can see, any special faculty of intuition for its apprehension. It is neither intellect nor intuition, but sensation, that supplies new data; but when the data are new in any remarkable manner, intellect is much more capable of dealing with them than intuition would be. The hen with a brood of ducklings no doubt has intuition which seems to place her inside them, and not merely to know them analytically; but when the ducklings take to the water, the whole apparent intuition is seen to be illusory, and the hen is left helpless on the shore. Intuition, in fact, is an aspect and development of instinct, and, like all instinct, is admirable in those customary surroundings which have moulded the habits of the animal in question, but totally incompetent as soon as the surroundings are changed in a way which demands some non-habitual mode of action.

The theoretical understanding of the world, which is the aim of philosophy, is not a matter of great practical importance to animals, or to savages, or even to most civilized men. It is hardly to be supposed, therefore, that the rapid, rough and ready methods of instinct or intuition will find in this field a favourable ground for their application. It is the older kinds of activity, which bring out our kinship with remote generations of animal and semi-human ancestors, that show intuition at its best. In such matters as self-preservation and love, intuition will act sometimes (though not always) with a swiftness and precision which are astonishing to the critical intellect. But philosophy is not one of the pursuits which illustrate our affinity with the past: it is a highly refined, highly civilized pursuit, demanding, for its success, a certain liberation from the life of instinct, and even, at times, a certain aloofness from all mundane hopes and fears. It is not in philosophy, therefore, that we can hope to see intuition at its best. On the contrary, since the true objects of philosophy, and the habit of thought demanded for their apprehension, are strange, unusual, and remote, it is here, more almost than anywhere else, that intellect proves superior to intuition, and that quick unanalysed convictions are least deserving of uncritical acceptance.

In advocating the scientific restraint and balance, as against the self-assertion of a confident reliance upon intuition, we are only urging, in the sphere of knowledge, that largeness of contemplation, that impersonal disinterestedness, and that freedom from practical preoccupations which have been inculcated by all the great religions of the world. Thus our conclusion, however it may conflict with the explicit beliefs of many mystics, is, in essence, not contrary to the spirit which inspires those beliefs, but rather the outcome of this very spirit as applied in the realm of thought.

II. UNITY AND PLURALITY

One of the most convincing aspects of the mystic illumination is the apparent revelation of the oneness of all things, giving rise to pantheism in religion and to monism in philosophy. An elaborate logic, beginning with Parmenides, and culminating in Hegel and his followers, has been gradually developed, to prove that the universe is one indivisible Whole, and that what seems to be its parts, if considered as substantial and self-existing, are mere illusion. The conception of a Reality quite other than the world of appearance, a reality one, indivisible, and unchanging, was introduced into Western philosophy by Parmenides, not, nominally at least, for mystical or religious reasons, but on the basis of a logical argument as to the impossibility of not-being, and most subsequent metaphysical systems are the outcome of this fundamental idea.

The logic used in defence of mysticism seems to be faulty as logic, and open to technical criticisms, which I have explained elsewhere. I shall not here repeat these criticisms, since they are lengthy and difficult, but shall instead attempt an analysis of the state of mind from which mystical logic has arisen.

Belief in a reality quite different from what appears to the senses arises with irresistible force in certain moods, which are the source of most mysticism, and of most metaphysics. While such a mood is dominant, the need of logic is not felt, and accordingly the more thorough-going mystics do not employ logic, but appeal directly to the immediate deliverance of their insight. But such fully developed mysticism is rare in the West. When the intensity of emotional conviction subsides, a man who is in the habit of reasoning will search for logical grounds in favour of the belief which he finds in himself. But since the belief already exists, he will be very hospitable to any ground that suggests itself. The paradoxes apparently proved by his logic are really the paradoxes of mysticism, and are the goal which he feels his logic must reach if it is to be in accordance with insight. The resulting logic has rendered most philosophers incapable of giving any account of the world of science and daily life. If they had been anxious to give such an account, they would probably have discovered the errors of their logic; but most of them were less anxious to understand the world of science and daily life than to convict it of unreality in the interests of a super-sensible 'real' world.

It is in this way that logic has been pursued by those of the great philosophers who were mystics. But since they usually took for granted the supposed insight of the mystic emotion, their logical doctrines were presented with a certain dryness, and were believed by their disciples to be quite independent of the sudden illumination from which they sprang. Nevertheless their origin clung to them, and they remained -- to borrow a useful word from Mr. Santayana -- 'malicious' in regard to the world of science and common sense. It is only so that we can account for the complacency with which philosophers have accepted the inconsistency of their doctrines with all the common and scientific facts which seem best established and most worthy of belief.

The logic of mysticism shows, as is natural, the defects which are inherent in anything malicious. The impulse to logic, not felt while the mystic mood is dominant, reasserts itself as the mood fades, but with a desire to retain the vanishing insight, or at least to prove that it was insight, and that what seems to contradict it is illusion. The logic which thus arises is not quite disinterested or candid, and is inspired by a certain hatred of the daily world to which it is to be applied. Such an attitude naturally does not tend to the best results. Everyone knows that to read an author simply in order to refute him is not the way to understand him; and to read the book of Nature with a conviction that it is all illusion is just as unlikely to lead to understanding. If our logic is to find the common world intelligible, it must not be hostile, but must be inspired by a genuine acceptance such as is not usually to be found among metaphysicians.

III. TIME

The unreality of time is a cardinal doctrine of many metaphysical systems, often nominally based, as already by Parmenides, upon logical arguments, but originally derived, at any rate in the founders of new systems, from the certainty which is born in the moment of mystic insight. As a Persian Sufi poet says:

'Past and future are what veil God from our sight.

Burn up both of them with fire! How long

Wilt thou be partitioned by these segments as a reed?'[5]

The belief that what is ultimately real must be immutable is a very common one: it gave rise to the metaphysical notion of substance, and finds, even now, a wholly illegitimate satisfaction in such scientific doctrines as the conservation of energy and mass.

It is difficult to disentangle the truth and the error in this view. The arguments for the contention that time is unreal and that the world of sense is

---

[5] Whinfield's translation of the *Masnavi* (Trubner, 1887), p. 34.

illusory must, I think, be regarded as fallacious. Nevertheless there is some sense -- easier to feel than to state -- in which time is an unimportant and superficial characteristic of reality. Past and future must be acknowledged to be as real as the present, and a certain emancipation from slavery to time is essential to philosophic thought. The importance of time is rather practical than theoretical, rather in relation to our desires than in relation to truth. A truer image of the world, I think, is obtained by picturing things as entering into the stream of time from an eternal world outside, than from a view which regards time as the devouring tyrant of all that is. Both in thought and in feeling, even though time be real, to realize the unimportance of time is the gate of wisdom.

That this is the case may be seen at once by asking ourselves why our feelings towards the past are so different from our feelings towards the future. The reason for this difference is wholly practical: our wishes can affect the future but not the past, the future is to some extent subject to our power, while the past is unalterably fixed. But every future will some day be past: if we see the past truly now, it must, when it was still future, have been just what we now see it to be, and what is now future must be just what we shall see it to be when it has become past. The felt difference of quality between past and future, therefore, is not an intrinsic difference, but only a difference in relation to us: to impartial contemplation, it ceases to exist. And impartiality of contemplation is, in the intellectual sphere, that very same virtue of disinterestedness which, in the sphere of action, appears as justice and unselfishness. Whoever wishes to see the world truly, to rise in thought above the tyranny of practical desires, must learn to overcome the difference of attitude towards past and future, and to survey the whole stream of time in one comprehensive vision.

The kind of way in which, as it seems to me, time ought not to enter into our theoretic philosophical thought, may be illustrated by the philosophy which has become associated with the idea of evolution, and which is exemplified by Nietzsche, pragmatism, and Bergson. This philosophy, on the basis of the development which has led from the lowest forms of life up to man, sees in progress the fundamental law of the universe, and thus admits the difference between *earlier* and *later* into the very citadel of its contemplative outlook. With its past and future history of the world, conjectural as it is, I do not wish to quarrel. But I think that, in the intoxication of a quick success, much that is required for a true understanding of the universe has been forgotten. Something of Hellenism, something, too, of Oriental resignation, must be combined with its hurrying Western self-assertion before it can emerge from the ardour of youth into the mature wisdom of manhood. In spite of its appeals to science, the true scientific philosophy, I think, is something more arduous and more aloof, appealing to less mundane hopes, and requiring a severer discipline for its successful practice.

Darwin's *Origin of Species* persuaded the world that the difference between different species of animals and plants is not the fixed immutable difference that it appears to be. The doctrine of natural kinds, which had rendered classification easy and definite, which was enshrined in the Aristotelian tradition, and protected by its supposed necessity for orthodox dogma, was suddenly swept away for ever out of the biological world. The difference between man and the lower animals, which to our human conceit appears enormous, was shown to be a gradual achievement, involving intermediate beings who could not with certainty be placed either within or without the human family. The sun and the planets had already been shown by Laplace to be very probably derived from a primitive more or less undifferentiated nebula. Thus the old fixed landmarks became wavering and indistinct, and all sharp outlines were blurred. Things and species lost their boundaries, and none could say where they began or where they ended.

But if human conceit was staggered for a moment by its kinship with the ape, it soon found a way to reassert itself, and that way is the 'philosophy' of evolution. A process which led from the amoeba to Man appeared to the philosophers to be obviously a progress -- though whether the amoeba would agree with this opinion is not known. Hence the cycle of changes which science had shown to be the probable history of the past was welcomed as revealing a law of development towards good in the universe -- an evolution or unfolding of an idea slowly embodying itself in the actual. But such a view, though it might satisfy Spencer and those whom we may call Hegelian evolutionists, could not be accepted as adequate by the more whole-hearted votaries of change. An ideal to which the world continuously approaches is, to these minds, too dead and static to be inspiring. Not only the aspiration, but the ideal too, must change and develop with the course of evolution: there must be no fixed goal, but a continual fashioning of fresh needs by the impulse which is life and which alone gives unity to the process.

Life, in this philosophy, is a continuous stream, in which all divisions are artificial and unreal. Separate things, beginnings and endings, are mere convenient fictions: there is only smooth unbroken transition. The beliefs of today may count as true today, if they carry us along the stream; but tomorrow they will be false, and must be replaced by new beliefs to meet the new situation. All our thinking consists of convenient fictions, imaginary congealings of the stream: reality flows on in spite of all our fictions, and though it can be lived, it cannot be conceived in thought. Somehow, without explicit statement, the assurance is slipped in that the future, though we cannot foresee it, will be better than the past or the present: the reader is like the child which expects a sweet because it has been told to open its mouth and shut its eyes. Logic, mathematics, physics disappear in this philosophy, because they are too static what is real is no impulse and movement towards a goal which, like the rainbow, recedes as we advance, and makes every place different when it reaches it from what it appeared to be at a distance.

I do not propose to enter upon a technical examination of this philosophy. I wish only to maintain that the motives and interests which inspire it are so exclusively practical, and the problems with which it deals are so special, that it can hardly be regarded as touching any of the questions that, to my mind, constitute genuine philosophy.

The predominant interest of evolutionism is in the question of human destiny, or at least of the destiny of Life. It is more interested in morality and happiness than in knowledge for its own sake. It must be admitted that the same may be said of many other philosophies, and that a desire for the kind of knowledge which philosophy can give is very rare. But if philosophy is to attain truth, it is necessary first and foremost that philosophers should acquire the disinterested intellectual curiosity which characterizes the genuine man of science. Knowledge concerning the future -- which is the kind of knowledge that must be sought if we are to know about human destiny -- is possible within certain narrow limits. It is impossible to say how much the limits may be enlarged with the progress of science. But what is evident is that any proposition about the future belongs by its subject-matter to some particular science, and is to be ascertained, if at all, by the methods of that science. Philosophy is not a short cut to the same kind of results as those of the other sciences: if it is to be a genuine study, it must have a province of its own, and aim at results which the other sciences can neither prove nor disprove.

Evolutionism, in basing itself upon the notion of *progress,* which is change from the worse to the better, allows the notion of time, as it seems to me, to become its tyrant rather than its servant, and thereby loses that impartiality of contemplation which is the source of all that is best in philosophic thought and feeling. Metaphysicians, as we saw, have frequently denied altogether the reality of time. I do not wish to do this; I wish only to preserve the mental outlook which inspired the denial, the attitude which, in thought, regards the past as having the same reality as the present and the same importance as the future. 'In so far,' says Spinoza[6] 'as the mind conceives a thing according to the dictate of reason, it will be equally affected whether the idea is that of a future, past, or present thing.' It is this 'conceiving according to the dictate of reason' that I find lacking in the philosophy which is based on evolution.

---

[6] *Ethics,* Bk. IV, Prop. LXII.

IV. GOOD AND EVIL

Mysticism maintains that all evil is illusory, and sometimes maintains the same view as regards good, but more often holds that all Reality is good. Both views are to be found in Heraclitus: 'Good and ill are one,' he says, but again, 'To God all things are fair and good and right, but men hold some things wrong and some right.' A similar twofold position is to be found in Spinoza, but he uses the word 'perfection' when he means to speak of the good that is not merely human. 'By reality and perfection I mean the same thing,' he says;[7] but elsewhere we find the definition: 'By *good* I shall mean that which we certainly know to be useful to us.'[8] Thus perfection belongs to Reality in its own nature, but goodness is relative to ourselves and our needs, and disappears in an impartial survey. Some such distinction, I think, is necessary in order to understand the ethical outlook of mysticism: there is a lower mundane kind of good and evil, which divides the world of appearance into what seem to be conflicting parts; but there is also a higher, mystical kind of good, which belongs to Reality and is not opposed by any correlative kind of evil.

It is difficult to give a logically tenable account of this position without recognizing that good and evil are subjective, that what is good is merely that towards which we have one kind of feeling, and what is evil is merely that towards which we have another kind of feeling. In our active life, where we have to exercise choice, and to prefer this to that of two possible acts, it is necessary to have a distinction of good and evil, or at least of better and worse. But this distinction, like everything pertaining to action, belongs to what mysticism regards as the world of illusion, if only because it is essentially concerned with time. In our contemplative life, where action is not called for, it is possible to be impartial, and to overcome the ethical dualism which action requires. So long as we remain *merely* impartial, we may be content to say that both the good and the evil of action are illusions. But if, as we must do if we have the mystic vision, we find the whole world worthy of love and worship, if we see

'The earth, and every common sight. . .

Apparell'd in celestial light,'

we shall say that there is a higher good than that of action, and that this higher good belongs to the whole world as it is in reality. In this way the twofold attitude and the apparent vacillation of mysticism are explained and justified.

---

[7] Ib., Pt. IV, Df. I.

[8] Ethics, Pt. II, Df. VI.

The possibility of this universal love and joy in all that exists is of supreme importance for the conduct and happiness of life, and gives inestimable value to the mystic emotion, apart from any creeds which may be built upon it. But if we are not to be led into false beliefs, it is necessary to realize exactly *what* the mystic emotion reveals. It reveals a possibility of human nature -- a possibility of a nobler, happier, freer life than any that can be otherwise achieved. But it does not reveal anything about the non-human, or about the nature of the universe in general. Good and bad, and even the higher good that mysticism finds everywhere, are the reflections of our own emotions on other things, not part of the substance of things as they are in themselves. And therefore an impartial contemplation, freed from all preoccupation with Self, will not judge things good or bad, although it is very easily combined with that feeling of universal love which leads the mystic to say that the whole world is good.

The philosophy of evolution, through the notion of progress, is bound up with the ethical dualism of the worse and the better, and is thus shut out, not only from the kind of survey which discards good and evil altogether from its view, but also from the mystical belief in the goodness of everything. In this way the distinction of good and evil, like time, becomes a tyrant in this philosophy, and introduces into thought the restless selectiveness of action. Good and evil, like time, are, it would seem, not general or fundamental in the world of thought, but late and highly specialized members of the intellectual hierarchy.

Although, as we saw, mysticism can be interpreted so as to agree with the view that good and evil are not intellectually fundamental, it must be admitted that here we are no longer in verbal agreement with most of the great philosophers and religious teachers of the past. I believe, however, that the elimination of ethical considerations from philosophy is both scientifically necessary and -- though this may seem a paradox -- an ethical advance. Both these contentions must be briefly defended.

The hope of satisfaction to our more human desires -- the hope of demonstrating that the world has this or that desirable ethical characteristic -- is not one which, so far as I can see, a scientific philosophy can do anything whatever to satisfy. The difference between a good world and a bad one is a difference in the particular characteristics of the particular things that exist in these worlds: it is not a sufficiently abstract difference to come within the province of philosophy. Love and hate, for example, are ethical opposites, but to philosophy they are closely analogous attitudes towards objects. The general form and structure of those attitudes towards objects which constitute mental phenomena is a problem for philosophy, but the difference between love and hate is not a difference of form or structure, and therefore belongs rather to the special science of psychology than to philosophy. Thus the ethical interests which have often inspired philosophers must remain in the background: some kind of ethical interest may inspire the whole study, but none must obtrude in the detail or be expected in the special results which are sought.

If this view seems at first sight disappointing, we may remind ourselves that a similar change has been found necessary in all the other sciences. The physicist or chemist is not now required to prove the ethical importance of his ions or atoms; the biologist is not expected to prove the utility of the plants or animals which he dissects. In pre-scientific ages this was not the case. Astronomy, for example, was studied because men believed in astrology: it was thought that the movements of the planets had the most direct and important bearing upon the lives of human beings. Presumably, when this belief decayed and the disinterested study of astronomy begin, many who had found astrology absorbingly interesting decided that astronomy had too little human interest to be worthy of study. Physics, as it appears in Plato's Timaeus for example, is full of ethical notions: it is an essential part of its purpose to show that the earth is worthy of admiration. The modern physicist, on the contrary, though he has no wish to deny that the earth is admirable, is not concerned, as physicist, with its ethical attributes: he is merely concerned to find out facts, not to consider whether they are good or bad. In psychology, the scientific attitude is even more recent and more difficult than in the physical sciences: it is natural to consider that human nature is either good or bad, and to suppose that the difference between good and bad, so all-important in practice, must be important in theory also. It is only during the last century that an ethically neutral psychology has grown up; and here too, ethical neutrality has been essential to scientific success.

In philosophy, hitherto, ethical neutrality has been seldom sought and hardly ever achieved. Men have remembered their wishes, and have judged philosophies in relation to their wishes. Driven from the particular sciences, the belief that the notions of good and evil must afford a key to the understanding of the world has sought a refuge in philosophy. But even from this last refuge, if philosophy is not to remain a set of pleasing dreams, this belief must be driven forth. It is a commonplace that happiness is not best achieved by those who seek it directly; and it would seem that the same is true of the good. In thought, at any rate, those who forget good and evil and seek only to know the facts are more likely to achieve good than those who view the world through the distorting medium of their own desires.

We are thus brought back to our seeming paradox, that a philosophy which does not seek to impose upon the world its own conceptions of good and evil is not only more likely to achieve truth, but is also the outcome of a higher ethical standpoint than one which, like evolutionism and most traditional systems, is perpetually appraising the universe and seeking to find in it an embodiment of present ideals. In religion, and in every deeply serious view of the world and of human destiny, there is an element of submission, a realization of the limits of human power, which is somewhat lacking in the modern world, with its quick material successes and its insolent belief in the boundless possibilities of progress. 'He that loveth his life shall lose it;' and there is danger lest, through a too confident love of life, life itself should lose much of what gives it its highest worth. The submission which religion inculcates in action is essentially the same in spirit as that which science teaches in thought; and the ethical neutrality by which its victories have been achieved is the outcome of that submission.

The good which it concerns us to remember is the good which it lies in our power to create -- the good in our own lives and in our attitude towards the world. Insistence on belief in an external realization of the good is a form of self-assertion, which, while it cannot secure the external good which it desires, can seriously impair the inward good which lies within our power, and destroy that reverence towards fact which constitutes both what is valuable in humility and what is fruitful in the scientific temper.

Human beings cannot, of course, wholly transcend human nature; something subjective, if only the interest that determines the direction of our attention, must remain in all our thought. But scientific philosophy comes nearer to objectivity than any other human pursuit, and gives us, therefore, the closest constant and the most intimate relation with the outer world that it is possible to achieve. To the primitive mind, everything is either friendly or hostile; but experience has shown that friendliness and hostility are not the conceptions by which the world is to be understood. Scientific philosophy thus represents, though as yet only in a nascent condition, a higher form of thought than any pre-scientific belief or imagination, and, like every approach to self-transcendence, it brings with it a rich reward in increase of scope and breadth and comprehension. Evolutionism, in spite of its appeals to particular scientific facts, fails to be a truly scientific philosophy because of its slavery to time, its ethical preoccupations, and its predominant interest in our mundane concerns and destiny. A truly scientific philosophy will be more humble, more piecemeal, more arduous, offering less glitter of outward mirage to flatter fallacious hopes, but more indifferent to fate, and more capable of accepting the world without the tyrannous imposition of our human and temporary demands.

THE PLACE OF SCIENCE IN A LIBERAL EDUCATION

SCIENCE, to the ordinary reader of newspapers, is represented by a varying selection of sensational triumphs, such as wireless telegraphy and aeroplanes, radio-activity and the marvels of modern alchemy. It is not of this aspect of science that I wish to speak. Science, in this aspect, consists of detached up-to-date fragments, interesting only until they are replaced by something newer and more up-to-date, displaying nothing of the systems of patiently constructed knowledge out of which, almost as a casual incident, have come the practically useful results which interest the man in the street. The increased command over the forces of nature which is derived from science is undoubtedly an amply sufficient reason for encouraging scientific research, but this reason has been so often urged and is so easily appreciated that other reasons, to my mind quite as important, are apt to be overlooked. It is with these other reasons, especially with the intrinsic value of a scientific habit of mind in forming our outlook on the world, that I shall be concerned in what follows.

The instance of wireless telegraphy will serve to illustrate the difference between the two points of view. Almost all the serious intellectual labour required for the possibility of this invention is due to three men -- Faraday, Maxwell, and Hertz. In alternating layers of experiment and theory these three men built up the modern theory of electromagnetism, and demonstrated the identity of light with electromagnetic waves. The system which they discovered is one of profound intellectual interest, bringing together and unifying an endless variety of apparently detached phenomena, and displaying a cumulative mental power which cannot but afford delight to every generous spirit. The mechanical details which remained to be adjusted in order to utilize their discoveries for a practical system of telegraphy demanded, no doubt, very considerable ingenuity, but had not that broad sweep and that universality which could give them instrinsic interest as an object of disinterested contemplation.

From the point of view of training the mind, of giving that well-informed, impersonal outlook which constitutes culture in the good sense of this much-misused word, it seems to be generally held indisputable that a literary education is superior to one based on science. Even the warmest advocates of science are apt to rest their claims on the contention that culture ought to be sacrificed to utility. Those men of science who respect culture, when they associate with men learned in the classics, are apt to admit, not merely politely, but sincerely, a certain inferiority on their side, compensated doubtless by the services which science renders to humanity, but none the less real. And so long as this attitude exists among men of science, it tends to verify itself: the intrinsically valuable aspects of science tend to be sacrificed to the merely useful, and little attempt is made to preserve that leisurely, systematic survey by which the finer quality of mind is formed and nourished.

But even if there be, in present fact, any such inferiority as is supposed in the educational value of science, this is, I believe, not the fault of science itself, but the fault of the spirit in which science is taught. If its full possibilities were realized by those who teach it, I believe that its capacity of producing those habits of mind which constitute the highest mental excellence would be at least as great as that of literature, and more particularly of Greek and Latin literature. In saying this I have no wish whatever to disparage a classical education. I have not myself enjoyed its benefits, and my knowledge of Greek and Latin authors is derived almost wholly from translations. But I am firmly persuaded that the Greeks fully deserve all the admiration that is bestowed upon them, and that it is a very great and serious loss to be unacquainted with their writings. It is not by attacking them, but by drawing attention to neglected excellences in science, that I wish to conduct my argument.

One defect, however, does seem inherent in a purely classical education -- namely, a too exclusive emphasis on the past. By the study of what is absolutely ended and can never be renewed, a habit of criticism towards the present and the future is engendered. The qualities in which the present excels are qualities to which the study of the past does not direct attention, and to which, therefore, the student of Greek civilization may easily become blind. In what is new and growing there is apt to be something crude, insolent, even a little vulgar, which is shocking to the man of sensitive taste; quivering from the rough contact, he retires to the trim gardens of a polished past, forgetting that they were reclaimed from the wilderness by men as rough and earth-soiled as those from whom he shrinks in his own day. The habit of being unable to recognize merit until it is dead is too apt to be the result of a purely bookish life, and a culture based wholly on the past will seldom be able to pierce through everyday surroundings to the essential splendour of contemporary things, or to the hope of still greater splendour in the future.

> 'My eyes saw not the men of old;
> And now their age away has rolled.
> I weep -- to think I shall not see
> The heroes of posterity.'

So says the Chinese poet; but such impartiality is rare in the more pugnacious atmosphere of the West, where the champions of past and future fight a never-ending battle, instead of combining to seek out the merits of both.

This consideration, which militates not only against the exclusive study of the classics, but against every form of culture which has become static, traditional, and academic, leads inevitably to the fundamental question: What is the true end of education? But before attempting to answer this question it will be well to define the sense in which we are to use the word 'education'. For this purpose I shall distinguish the sense in which I mean to use it from two others, both perfectly legitimate, the one broader and the other narrower than the sense in which I mean to use the word.

In the broader sense, education will include not only what we learn through instruction, but all that we learn through personal experience -- the formation of character through the education of life. Of this aspect of education, vitally important as it is, I will say nothing, since its consideration would introduce topics quite foreign to the question with which we are concerned.

In the narrower sense, education may be confined to instruction, the imparting of definite information on various subjects, because such information, in and for itself, is useful in daily life. Elementary education -- reading, writing, and arithmetic -- is almost wholly of this kind. But instruction, necessary as it is, does not *per se* constitute education in the sense in which I wish to consider it.

Education, in the sense in which I mean it, may be defined as *the formation, by means of instruction, of certain mental habits and a certain outlook on life and the world.* It remains to ask ourselves, what mental habits, and what sort of outlook, can be hoped for as the result of instruction? When we have answered this question we can attempt to decide what science has to contribute to the formation of the habits and outlook which we desire.

Our whole life is built about a certain number -- not a very small number -- of primary instincts and impulses. Only what is in some way connected with these instincts and impulses appears to us desirable or important; there is no faculty, whether reason or 'virtue' or whatever it may be called, that can take our active life and our hopes and fears outside the region controlled by these first movers of all desire. Each of them is like a queen bee, aided by a hive of workers gathering honey; but when the queen is gone the workers languish and die, and the cells remain empty of their expected sweetness. So with each primary impulse in civilized man: it is surrounded and protected by a busy swarm of attendant derivative desires, which store up in its service whatever honey the surrounding world affords. But if the queen-impulse dies, the death-dealing influence, though retarded a little by habit, spreads slowly through all the subsidiary impulses, and a whole tract of life becomes inexplicably colourless. What was formerly full of zest, and so obviously worth doing that it raised no questions, has now grown dreary and purposeless: with a sense of disillusion we inquire the meaning of life, and decide, perhaps, that all is vanity. The search for an outside meaning that can *compel* an inner response must always be disappointed: all 'meaning' must be at bottom related to our primary desires, and when they are extinct no miracle can restore to the world the value which they reflected upon it.

The purpose of education, therefore, cannot be to create any primary impulse which is lacking in the uneducated; the purpose can only be to enlarge the scope of those that human nature provides, by increasing the number and variety of attendant thoughts, and by showing where the most permanent satisfaction is to be found. Under the impulse of a Calvinistic horror of the 'natural man', this obvious truth has been too often misconceived in the training of the young; 'nature' has been falsely regarded as excluding all that is best in what is natural, and the endeavour to teach virtue has led to the production of stunted and contorted hypocrites instead of full-grown human beings. From such mistakes in education a better psychology or a kinder heart is beginning to preserve the present generation; we need, therefore, waste no more words on the theory that the purpose of education is to thwart or eradicate nature.

But although nature must supply the initial force of desire, nature is not, in the civilized man, the spasmodic, fragmentary, and yet violent set of impulses that it is in the savage. Each impulse has its constitutional ministry of thought and knowledge and reflection, through which possible conflicts of impulses are foreseen, and temporary impulses are controlled by the unifying impulse which may be called wisdom. In this way education destroys the crudity of instinct, and increases through knowledge the wealth and variety of the individual's contacts with the outside world, making him no longer an isolated fighting unit, but a citizen of the universe, embracing distant countries, remote regions of space, and vast stretches of past and future within the circle of his interests. It is this simultaneous softening in the insistence of desire and enlargement of its scope that is the chief moral end of education.

Closely connected with this moral end is the more purely intellectual aim of education, the endeavour to make us see and imagine the world in an objective manner, as far as possible as it is in itself, and not merely through the distorting medium of personal desire. The complete attainment of such an objective view is no doubt an ideal, indefinitely approachable, but not actually and fully realizable. Education, considered as a process of forming our mental habits and our outlook on the world, is to be judged successful in proportion as its outcome approximates to this ideal; in proportion, that is to say, as it gives us a true view of our place in society, of the relation of the whole human society to its non-human environment, and of the nature of the non-human world as it is in itself apart from our desires and interests. If this standard is admitted, we can return to the consideration of science, inquiring how far science contributes to such an aim, and whether it is in any respect superior to its rivals in educational practice.

II

Two opposite and at first sight conflicting merits belong to science as against literature and art. The one, which is not inherently necessary, but is certainly true at the present day, is hopefulness as to the future of human achievement, and in particular as to the useful work that may be accomplished by any intelligent student. This merit and the cheerful outlook which it engenders prevent what might otherwise be the depressing effect of another aspect of science, to my mind also a merit, and perhaps its greatest merit -- I mean the irrelevance of human passions and of the whole subjective apparatus where scientific truth is concerned. Each of these reasons for preferring the study of science requires some amplification. Let us begin with the first.

In the study of literature or art our attention is perpetually riveted Upon the past: the men of Greece or of the Renaissance did better than any men do now; the triumphs of former ages, so far from facilitating fresh triumphs in our own age, actually increase the difficulty of fresh triumphs by rendering originality harder of attainment; not only is artistic achievement not cumulative, but it seems even to depend upon a certain freshness and *naivete* of impulse and vision which civilization tends to destroy. Hence comes, to those who have been nourished on the literary and artistic productions of former ages, a certain peevishness and undue fastidiousness towards the present, from which there seems no escape except into the deliberate vandalism which ignores tradition and in the search after originality achieves only the eccentric. But in such vandalism there is none of the simplicity and spontaneity out of which great art springs: theory is still the canker in its core, and insincerity destroys the advantages of a merely pretended ignorance.

The despair thus arising from an education which suggests no preeminent mental activity except that of artistic creation is wholly absent from an education which gives the knowledge of scientific method. The discovery of scientific method, except in pure mathematics, is a thing of yesterday; speaking broadly, we may say that it dates from Galileo. Yet already it has transformed the world, and its success proceeds with ever-accelerating velocity. In science men have discovered an activity of the very highest value in which they are no longer, as in art, dependent for progress upon the appearance of continually greater genius, for in science the successors stand upon the shoulders of their predecessors; where one man of supreme genius has invented a method, a thousand lesser men can apply it. No transcendent ability is required in order to make useful discoveries in science; the edifice of science needs its masons, bricklayers and common labourers as well as its foremen, master-builders and architects. In art nothing worth doing can be done without genius; in science even a very moderate capacity can contribute to a supreme achievement.

In science the man of real genius is the man who invents a new method. The notable discoveries are often made by his successors, who can apply the method with fresh vigour, unimpaired by the previous labour of perfecting it; but the mental calibre of the thought required for their work, however brilliant, is not so great as that required by the first inventor of the method. There are in science immense numbers of different methods, appropriate to different classes of problems; but over and above them all, there is something not easily definable, which may be called *the* method of science. It was formerly customary to identify this with the inductive method, and to associate it with the name of Bacon. But the true inductive method was not discovered by Bacon, and the true method of science is something which includes deduction as much as induction, logic and mathematics as much as botany and geology. I shall not attempt the difficult task of stating what the scientific method is, but I will try to indicate the temper of mind out of which the scientific method grows, which is the second of the two merits that were mentioned above as belonging to a scientific education.

The kernel of the scientific outlook is a thing so simple, so obvious, so seemingly trivial, that the mention of it may almost excite derision. The kernel of the scientific outlook is the refusal to regard our own desires, tastes and interests as affording a key to the understanding of the world. Stated thus baldly, this may seem no more than a trite truism. But to remember it consistently in matters arousing our passionate partisanship is by no means easy, especially where the available evidence is uncertain and inconclusive. A few illustrations will make this clear.

Aristotle, I understand, considered that the stars must move in circles because the circle is the most perfect curve. In the absence of evidence to the contrary, he allowed himself to decide a question of fact by an appeal to aesthetico-moral considerations. In such a case it is at once obvious to us that this appeal was unjustifiable. We know now how to ascertain as a fact the way in which the heavenly bodies move, and we know that they do not move in circles, or even in accurate ellipses, or in any other kind of simply describable curve. This may be painful to a certain hankering after simplicity of pattern in the universe, but we know that in astronomy such feelings are irrelevant. Easy as this knowledge seems now, we owe it to the courage and insight of the first inventors of scientific method, and more especially of Galileo.

We may take as another illustration Malthus's doctrine of population. This illustration is all the better for the fact that his actual doctrine is now known to be largely erroneous. It is not his conclusions that are valuable, but the temper and method of his inquiry. As everyone knows, it was to him that Darwin owed an essential part of his theory of natural selection, and this was only possible because Malthus's outlook was truly scientific. His great merit lies in considering man not as the object of praise or blame, but as a part of nature, a thing with a certain characteristic behaviour from which certain consequences must follow. If the behaviour is not quite what Malthus supposed, if the consequences are not quite what he inferred, that may falsify his conclusions, but does not impair the value of his method. The objections which were made when his doctrine was new -- that it was horrible and depressing, that people ought not to act as he said they did, and so on -- were all such as implied an unscientific attitude of mind; as against all of them, his calm determination to treat man as a natural phenomenon marks an important advance over the reformers of the eighteenth century and the Revolution.

Under the influence of Darwinism the scientific attitude towards man has now become fairly common, and is to some people quite natural, though to most it is still a difficult and artificial contortion. There is, however, one study which is as yet almost wholly untouched by the scientific spirit -- I mean the study of philosophy. Philosophers and the public imagine that the scientific spirit must pervade pages that bristle with allusions to ions, germ plasms, and the eyes of shellfish. But as the devil can quote Scripture, so the philosopher can quote science. The scientific spirit is not an affair of quotation, of externally acquired information, any more than manners are an affair of the etiquette book. The scientific attitude of mind involves a sweeping away of all other desires in the interests of the desire to know -- it involves suppression of hopes and fears, loves and hates, and the whole subjective emotional life, until we become subdued to the material, able to see it frankly, without preconceptions, without bias, without any wish except to see it as it is, and without any belief that what it is must be determined by some relation, positive or negative, to what we should like it to be, or to what we can easily imagine it to be.

Now in philosophy this attitude of mind has not as yet been achieved. A certain self-absorption, not personal, but human, has marked almost all attempts to conceive the universe as a whole. Mind, or some aspect of it -- thought or will or sentience -- has been regarded as the pattern after which the universe is to be conceived, for no better reason, at bottom, than that such a universe would not seem strange, and would give us the cosy feeling that every place is like home. To conceive the universe as essentially progressive or essentially deteriorating, for example, is to give to our hopes and fears a cosmic importance which *may*, of course, be justified, but which we have as yet no reason to suppose justified. Until we have learnt to think of it in ethically neutral terms, we have not arrived at a scientific attitude in philosophy; and until we have arrived at such an attitude, it is hardly to be hoped that philosophy will achieve any solid results.

I have spoken so far largely of the negative aspect of the scientific spirit, but it is from the positive aspect that its value is derived. The instinct of constructiveness, which is one of the chief incentives to artistic creation, can find in scientific systems a satisfaction more massive than any epic poem.

Disinterested curiosity, which is the source of almost all-intellectual effort, finds with astonished delight that science can unveil secrets which might well have seemed forever undiscoverable. The desire for a larger life and wider interests, for an escape from private circumstances, and even from the whole recurring human cycle of birth and death, is fulfilled by the impersonal cosmic outlook of science as by nothing else. To all these must be added, as contributing to the happiness of the man of science, the admiration of splendid achievement, and the consciousness of inestimable utility to the human race. A life devoted to science is therefore a happy life, and its happiness is derived from the very best sources that are open to dwellers on this troubled and passionate planet.

ON SCIENTIFIC METHOD IN PHILOSOPHY[1]

WHEN we try to ascertain the motives which have led men to the investigation of philosophical questions, we find that, broadly speaking, they can be divided into two groups, often antagonistic, and leading to very divergent systems. These two groups of motives are, on the one hand, those derived from religion and ethics, and, on the other hand, those derived from science. Plato, Spinoza, and Hegel may be taken as typical of the philosophers whose interests are mainly religious and ethical, while Leibniz, Locke, and Hume may be taken as representatives of the scientific wing. In Aristotle, Descartes, Berkeley, and Kant we find both groups of motives strongly present.

Herbert Spencer, in whose honour we are assembled today, would naturally be classed among scientific philosophers: it was mainly from science that he drew his data, his formulation of problems, and his conception of method. But his strong religious sense is obvious in much of his writing, and his ethical preoccupations are what make him value the conception of evolution -- that conception in which, as a whole generation has believed, science and morals are to be united in fruitful and indissoluble marriage.

It is my belief that the ethical and religious motives in spite of the splendidly imaginative systems to which they have given rise, have been on the whole a hindrance to the progress of philosophy, and ought now to be consciously thrust aside by those who wish to discover philosophical truth. Science, originally, was entangled in similar motives, and was thereby hindered in its advances. It is, I maintain, from science, rather than from ethics and religion, that philosophy should draw its inspiration.

But there are two different ways in which a philosophy may seek to base itself upon science. It may emphasize the most general *results* of science, and seek to give even greater generality and unity to these results. Or it may study the methods of science, and seek to apply those *methods*, with the necessary adaptations, to its own peculiar province. Much philosophy inspired by science has gone astray through preoccupation with the results momentarily supposed to have been achieved. It is not results, but methods, that can be transferred with profit from the sphere of the special sciences to the sphere of philosophy. What I wish to bring to your notice is the possibility and importance of applying to philosophical problems certain broad principles of method which have been found successful in the study of scientific questions.

---

[1] The Herbert Spencer lecture, Oxford, 1914.

The opposition between a philosophy guided by scientific method and a philosophy dominated by religious and ethical ideas may be illustrated by two notions which are very prevalent in the works of philosophers, namely the notion of the universe, and the notion of good and evil. A philosopher is expected to tell us something about the nature of the universe as a whole, and to give grounds for either optimism or pessimism. Both these expectations seem to me mistaken. I believe the conception of 'the universe' to be, as its etymology indicates, a mere relic of pre-Copernican astronomy: and I believe the question of optimism and pessimism to be one which the philosopher will regard as outside his scope, except, possibly, to the extent of maintaining that it is insoluble.

In the days before Copernicus, the conception of the 'universe' was defensible on scientific grounds: the diurnal revolution of the heavenly bodies bound them together as all parts of one system, of which the earth was the centre. Round this apparent scientific fact, many human desires rallied: the wish to believe Man important in the scheme of things, the theoretical desire for a comprehensive understanding of the Whole, the hope that the course of nature might be guided by some sympathy with our wishes. In this way, an ethically inspired system of metaphysics grew up, whose anthropocentrism was apparently warranted by the geocentrism of astronomy. When Copernicus swept away the astronomical basis of this system of thought, it had grown so familiar, and had associated itself so intimately with men's aspirations, that it survived with scarcely diminished force -- survived even Kant's 'Copernican revolution', and is still now the unconscious premise of most metaphysical systems.

The oneness of the world is an almost undiscussed postulate of most metaphysics. 'Reality is not merely one and self-consistent, but is a system of reciprocally determinate parts'[2] -- such a statement would pass almost unnoticed as a mere truism. Yet I believe that it embodies a failure to effect thoroughly the 'Copernican revolution', and that the apparent oneness of the world is merely the oneness of what is seen by a single spectator or apprehended by a single mind.

The Critical Philosophy, although it intended to emphasize the subjective element in many apparent characteristics of the world, yet, by regarding the world in itself as unknowable, so concentrated attention upon the subjective representation that its subjectivity was soon forgotten. Having recognized the categories as the work of the mind, it was paralysed by its own recognition, and abandoned in despair the attempt to undo the work of subjective falsification. In part, no doubt, its despair was well founded, but not, I think, in any absolute or ultimate sense. Still less was it a ground for rejoicing, or for supposing that the nescience to which it ought to have given rise could be legitimately exchanged for a metaphysical dogmatism.

---

[2] Bosanquet, *Logic*, ii. P.211.

I

As regards our present question, namely, the question of the unity of the world, the right method, as I think, has been indicated by William James.[3] "Let us now turn our backs upon ineffable or unintelligible ways of accounting for the world's oneness, and inquire whether, instead of being a principle, the "oneness" affirmed may not merely be a name like "substance" descriptive of the fact that certain specific and verifiable connections are found among the parts of the experiential flux. . . . We can easily conceive of things that shall have no connection whatever with each other. We may assume them to inhabit different times and spaces, as the dreams of different persons do even now. They may be so unlike and incommensurable, and so inert towards one another, as never to jostle or interfere. Even now there may actually be whole universes so disparate from ours that we who know ours have no means of perceiving that they exist. We conceive their diversity, however; and by that fact the whole lot of them form what is known in logic as "a universe of discourse". To form a universe of discourse argues, as this example shows, no further kind of connection. The importance attached by certain monistic writers to the fact that any chaos may become a universe by merely being named, is to me incomprehensible.' We are thus left with two kinds of unity in the experienced world; the one what we may call the epistemological unity, due merely to the fact that my experienced world is what one experience selects from the sum total of existence; the other that tentative and partial unity exhibited in the prevalence of scientific laws in those portions of the world which science has hitherto mastered. Now a generalization based upon either of these kinds of unity would be fallacious. That the things which we experience have the common property of being experienced by us is a truism from which obviously nothing of importance can be deducible: it is clearly fallacious to draw from the fact that whatever we experience is experienced the conclusion that therefore everything must be experienced. The generalization of the second kind of unity, namely, that derived from scientific laws, would be equally fallacious, though the fallacy is a trifle less elementary. In order to explain it let us consider for a moment what is called the reign of law. People often speak as though it were a remarkable fact that the physical world is subject to invariable laws. In fact, however, it is not easy to see how such a world could fail to obey general laws. Taking any arbitrary set of points in space, there is a function of the time corresponding to these points, i.e. expressing the motion of a particle which traverses these points: this function may be regarded as a general law to which the behaviour of such a particle is subject. Taking all such functions for all the particles in the universe, there will be theoretically some one formula embracing them all, and this formula may be regarded as the single and supreme law of the spatio-temporal world. Thus what is surprising in physics is not the existence of

---

[3] *Some Problems of Philosophy*, p.124

general laws, but their extreme simplicity. It is not the uniformity of nature that should surprise us, for, by sufficient analytic ingenuity, any conceivable course of nature might be shown to exhibit uniformity. What should surprise us is the fact that the uniformity is simple enough for us to be able to discover it. But it is just this characteristic of simplicity in the laws of nature hitherto discovered which it would be fallacious to generalize, for it is obvious that simplicity has been a part cause of their discovery, and can, therefore, give no ground for the supposition that other undiscovered laws are equally simple.

The fallacies to which these two kinds of unity have given rise suggest a caution as regards all use in philosophy of general results that science is supposed to have achieved. In the first place, in generalizing these results beyond past experience, it is necessary to examine very carefully whether there is not some reason making it more probable that these results should hold of all that has been experienced than that they should hold of things universally. The sum total of what is experienced by mankind is a selection from the sum total of what exists, and any general character exhibited by this selection may be due to the manner of selecting rather than to the general character of that from which experience selects. In the second place, the most general results of science are the least certain and the most liable to be upset by subsequent research. In utilizing these results as the basis of a philosophy, we sacrifice the most valuable and remarkable characteristic of scientific method, namely, that, although almost everything in science is found sooner or later to require some correction, yet this correction is almost always such as to leave untouched, or only slightly modified, the greater part of the results which have been deduced from the premise subsequently discovered to be faulty. The prudent man of science acquires a certain instinct as to the kind of uses which may be made of present scientific beliefs without incurring the danger of complete and utter refutation from the modifications likely to be introduced by subsequent discoveries. Unfortunately the use of scientific generalizations of a sweeping kind as the basis of philosophy is just that kind of use which an instinct of scientific caution would avoid, since, as a rule, it would only lead to true results if the generalization upon which it is based stood in no need of correction.

We may illustrate these general considerations by means of two examples, namely, the conservation of energy and the principle of evolution.

(1) Let us begin with the conservation of energy, or, as Herbert Spencer used to call it, the persistence of force. He says:[4]

---

[4] *First Principles* (1862), Part II, beginning of chap. viii.

'Before taking a first step in the rational interpretation of Evolution, it is needful to recognize, not only the facts that Matter is indestructible and Motion continuous, but also the fact that Force persists. An attempt to assign the *causes* of Evolution would manifestly be absurd if that agency to which the metamorphosis in general and in detail is due, could either come into existence or cease to exist. The succession of phenomena would in such case be altogether arbitrary, and deductive Science impossible.'

This paragraph illustrates the kind of way in which the philosopher is tempted to give an air of absoluteness and necessity to empirical generalizations, of which only the approximate truth in the regions hitherto investigated can be guaranteed by the unaided methods of science. It is very often said that the persistence of something or other is a necessary presupposition of all scientific investigation, and this presupposition is then thought to be exemplified in some quantity which physics declares to be constant. There are here, as it seems to me, three distinct errors. First, the detailed scientific investigation of nature does not presuppose any such general laws as its results are found to verify. Apart from particular observations, science need presuppose nothing except the general principles of logic, and these principles are not laws of nature, for they are merely hypothetical, and apply not only to the actual world but to whatever is possible. The second error consists in the identification of a constant quality with a persistent entity. Energy is a certain function of a physical system, but is not a thing or substance persisting throughout the changes of the system. The same is true of mass, in spite of the fact that mass has often been defined as quantity of matter. The whole conception, of quantity, involving, as it does, numerical measurement based largely upon conventions, is far more artificial, far more an embodiment of mathematical convenience, than is commonly believed by those who philosophize on physics. Thus even if (which I cannot for a moment admit) the persistence of some entity were among the necessary postulates of science, it would be a sheer error to infer from this the constancy of any physical quantity, or the *a priori* necessity of any such constancy which may be empirically discovered. In the third place, it has become more and more evident with the progress of physics that large generalizations, such as the conservation of energy or mass, are far from certain and are very likely only approximate. Mass, which used to be regarded as the most indubitable of physical quantities, is now generally believed to vary according to velocity, and to be, in fact, a vector quantity which at a given moment is different in different directions. The detailed conclusions deduced from the supposed constancy of mass for such motions as used to be studied in physics will remain very nearly exact, and therefore over the field of the older investigations very little modification of the older results is required. But as soon as such a principle as the conservation of mass or of energy is erected into a universal a *priori* law, the slightest failure in absolute exactness is fatal, and the whole philosophic structure raised upon this foundation is necessarily ruined. The prudent philosopher, therefore, though he may with advantage study the methods of physics, will be very chary of basing anything upon what happen at the moment to be the most general results apparently obtained by those methods.

(2) The philosophy of evolution, which was to be our second example, illustrates the same tendency to hasty generalization, and also another sort, namely, the undue preoccupation with ethical notions. There are two kinds of evolutionist philosophy, of which both Hegel and Spencer represent the older and less radical kind, while Pragmatism and Bergson represent the more modern and revolutionary variety. But both these sorts of evolutionism have in common the emphasis on progress, that is, upon a continual change from the worse to the better, or from the simpler to the more complex. It would be unfair to attribute to Hegel any scientific motive or foundation, but all the other evolutionists, including Hegel's modern disciples, have derived their impetus very largely from the history of biological development. To a philosophy which derives a law of universal progress from this history there are two objections. First, that this history itself is concerned with a very small selection of facts confined to an infinitesimal fragment of space and time, and even on scientific grounds probably not an average sample of events in the world at large. For we know that decay as well as growth is a normal occurrence m the world. An extra-terrestrial philosopher, who had watched a single youth up to the age of twenty-one and had never come across any other human being, might conclude that it is the nature of human beings to grow continually taller and wiser in an indefinite progress towards perfection; and this generalization would be just as well founded as the generalization which evolutionists base upon the previous history of this planet. Apart, however, from this scientific objection to evolutionism, there is another, derived from the undue admixture of ethical notions in the very idea of progress from which evolutionism derives its charm. Organic life, we are told) has developed gradually from the protozoon to the philosopher, and this development, we are assured, is indubitably an advance. Unfortunately it is the philosopher, not the protozoon, who gives us this assurance, and we can have no security that the impartial outsider would agree with the philosopher's self-complacent assumption. This point has been illustrated by the philosopher Chuang Tzu in the following instructive anecdote:

> 'The Grand Augur, in his ceremonial robes, approached the shambles and thus addressed the pigs: "How can you object to die? I shall fatten you for three months. I shall discipline myself for ten days and fast for three. I shall strew fine grass, and place you bodily upon a carved sacrificial dish. Does not this satisfy you?"

Then, speaking from the pigs' point of view, he continued:

> "It is better, perhaps, after all, to live on bran and escape the shambles...."

> "But then", added he, speaking from his own point of view, "to enjoy honour when alive one would readily die on a war-shield or in the headsman's basket."

> So he rejected the pigs' point of view and adopted his own point of view. In what sense, then, was he different from the pigs?'

I much fear that the evolutionists too often resemble the Grand Augur and the pigs.

The ethical element which has been prominent in many of the most famous systems of philosophy is, in my opinion, one of the most serious obstacles to the victory of scientific method in the investigation of philosophical questions. Human ethical notions, as Chuang Tzu perceived, are essentially anthropocentric, and involve, when used in metaphysics, an attempt, however veiled, to legislate for the universe on the basis of the present desires of men. In this way they interfere with that receptivity to fact which is the essence of the scientific attitude towards the world. To regard ethical notions as a key to the understanding of the world is essentially pre-Copernican. It is to make man, with the hopes and ideals which he happens to have at the present moment, the centre of the universe and the interpreter of its supposed aims and purposes. Ethical metaphysics is fundamentally an attempt, however disguised, to give legislative force to our own wishes. This may, of course, be questioned, but I think that it is confirmed by a consideration of the way in which ethical notions arise. Ethics is essentially a product of the gregarious instinct, that is to say, of the instinct to co-operate with those who are to form our own group against those who belong to other groups. Those who belong to our own group are good; those who belong to hostile groups are wicked. The ends which are pursued by our own group are desirable ends, the ends pursued by hostile groups are nefarious. The subjectivity of this situation is not apparent to the gregarious animal, which feels that the general principles of justice are on the side of its own herd. When the animal has arrived at the dignity of the metaphysician, it invents ethics as the embodiment of its belief in the justice of its own herd. So the Grand Augur invokes ethics as the justification of Augurs in their conflicts with pigs. But, it may be said, this view of ethics takes no account of such truly ethical notions as that of self-sacrifice. This, however, would be a mistake. The success of gregarious animals in the struggle for existence depends upon co-operation within the herd, and co-operation requires sacrifice, to some extent, of what would otherwise be the interests of the individual. Hence arises a conflict of desires and instincts, since both self-preservation and the preservation of the herd are biological ends to the individual. Ethics is in origin the art of recommending to others the sacrifices required for cooperation with oneself. Hence, by reflexion, it comes, through the operation of social justice, to recommend sacrifices by oneself, but all ethics, however refined, remains more or less subjective. Even vegetarians do not hesitate, for example, to save the life of a man in a fever, although in doing so they destroy the lives of many millions of microbes. The view of the world taken by the philosophy derived from ethical notions is thus never impartial and therefore never fully scientific. As compared with science, it fails to achieve the imaginative liberation from self which is necessary to such understanding of the world as man can hope to achieve, and the philosophy which it inspires is always more or less parochial, more or less infected with the prejudices of a time and a place.

I do not deny the importance or value, within its own sphere, of the kind of philosophy which is inspired by ethical notions. The ethical work of Spinoza, for example, appears to me of the very highest significance, but what is valuable in such work is not any metaphysical theory as to the nature of the world to which it may give rise, nor indeed anything which can be proved or disproved by argument. what is valuable is the indication of some new way of feeling towards life and the world, some way of feeling by which our own existence can acquire more of the characteristics which we must deeply desire. The value of such work, however immeasurable it is, belongs with practice and not with theory. Such theoretic importance as it may possess is only in relation to human nature, not in relation to the world at large. The scientific philosophy, therefore, which aims only at understanding the world and not directly at any other improvement of human life, cannot take account of ethical notions without being turned aside from that submission to fact which is the essence of the scientific temper.

II

If the notion of the universe and the notion of good and evil are extruded from scientific philosophy, it may be asked what specific problems remain for the philosopher as opposed to the man of science? It would be difficult to give a precise answer to this question, but certain characteristics may be noted as distinguishing the province of philosophy from that of the special sciences.

In the first place a philosophical proposition must be general. It must not deal specially with things on the surface of the earth, or with the solar system, or with any other portion of space and time. It is this need of generality which has led to the belief that philosophy deals with the universe as a whole. I do not believe that this belief is justified, but I do believe that a philosophical proposition must be applicable to everything that exists or may exist. It might be supposed that this admission would be scarcely distinguishable from the view which I wish to reject. This, however, would be an error, and an important one. The traditional view would make the universe itself the subject of various predicates which could not be applied to any particular thing in the universe, and the ascription of such peculiar predicates to the universe would be the special business of philosophy. I maintain, on the contrary, that there are no propositions of which the 'universe' is the subject; in other words, that there is no such thing as the 'universe'. What I do maintain is that there are general propositions which may be asserted of each individual thing, such as the propositions of logic. This does not involve that all the things there are form a whole which could be regarded as another thing and be made the subject of predicates. It involves only the assertion that there are properties which belong to each separate thing, not that there are properties belonging to the whole of things collectively. The philosophy which I wish to advocate may be called logical atomism or absolute pluralism, because, while maintaining that there are many things, it denies that there is a whole composed of those things. We shall see, therefore, that philosophical propositions, instead of being concerned with the whole of things collectively, are concerned with all things distributively; and not only must they be concerned with all things, but they must be concerned with such properties of all things as do not depend upon the accidental nature of the things that there happen to be, but are true of any possible world, independently of such facts as can only be discovered by our senses.

This brings us to a second characteristic of philosophical propositions, namely, that they must be a *priori*. A philosophical proposition must be such as can be neither proved nor disproved by empirical evidence. Too often we find in philosophical books arguments based upon the course of history, or the convolutions of the brain, or the eyes of shellfish. Special and accidental facts of this kind are irrelevant to philosophy, which must make only such assertions as would be equally true however the actual world were constituted.

We may sum up these two characteristics of philosophical propositions by saying that philosophy is the science of the possible. But this statement unexplained is liable to be misleading, since it may be thought that the possible is something other than the general, whereas in fact the two are indistinguishable.

Philosophy, if what has been said is correct, becomes indistinguishable from logic as that word has now come to be used. The study of logic consists, broadly speaking, of two not very sharply distinguished portions. On the one hand it is concerned with those general statements which can be made concerning everything without mentioning any one thing or predicate or relation, such for example as 'if X is a member of the class a and every member of a is a member of B, then X is a member of the class B, whatever X, A, and B may be.'

On the other hand, it is concerned with the analysis and enumeration of logical forms, i.e. with the kinds of propositions that may occur, with the various types of facts, and with the classification of the constituents of facts. In this way logic provides an inventory of possibilities, a repertory of abstractly tenable hypotheses.

It might be thought that such a study would be too vague and too general to be of any very great importance, and that, if its problems became at any point sufficiently definite, they would be merged in the problems of some special science. It appears, however, that this is not the case. In some problems, for example, the analysis of space and time, the nature of perception, or the theory of judgment, the discovery of the logical form of the facts involved is the hardest part of the work and the part whose performance has been most lacking hitherto. It is chiefly for want of the right logical hypothesis that such problems have hitherto been treated in such an unsatisfactory manner, and have given rise to those contradictions or antinomies in which the enemies of reason among philosophers have at all times delighted.

By concentrating attention upon the investigation of logical forms, it becomes possible at last for philosophy to deal with its problems piecemeal, and to obtain, as the sciences do, such partial and probably not wholly correct results as subsequent investigation can utilize even while it supplements and improves them. Most philosophies hitherto have been constructed all in one block, in such a way that, if they were not wholly correct, they were wholly incorrect, and could not be used as a basis for further investigations. It is chiefly owing to this fact that philosophy, unlike science, has hitherto been unprogressive, because each original philosopher has had to begin the work again from the beginning, without being able to accept anything definite from the work of his predecessors. A scientific philosophy such as I wish to recommend will be piecemeal and tentative like other sciences; above all, it will be able to invent hypotheses which, even if they are not wholly true, will yet remain fruitful after the necessary corrections have been made. This possibility of successive approximations to the truth is, more than anything else, the source of the triumphs of science, and to transfer this possibility to philosophy is to ensure a progress in method whose importance it would be almost impossible to exaggerate.

The essence of philosophy as thus conceived is analysis, not synthesis. To build up systems of the world, like Heine's German professor who knit together fragments of life and made an intelligible system out of them, is not, I believe, any more feasible than the discovery of the philosopher's stone. what is feasible is the understanding of general forms, and the division of traditional problems into a number of separate and less baffling questions. 'Divide and conquer' is the maxim of success here as elsewhere.

Let us illustrate these somewhat general maxims by examining their application to the philosophy of space, for it is only in application that the meaning or importance of a method can be understood. Suppose we are confronted with the problem of space as presented in Kant's Transcendental Aesthetic, and suppose we wish to discover what are the elements of the problem and what hope there is of obtaining a solution of them. It will soon appear that three entirely distinct problems, belonging to different studies, and requiring different methods for their solution, have been confusedly combined in the supposed single problem with which Kant is concerned. There is a problem of logic, a problem of physics, and a problem of theory of knowledge. Of these three, the problem of logic can be solved exactly and perfectly; the problem of physics can probably be solved with as great a degree of certainty and as great an approach to exactness as can be hoped in an empirical region; the problem of theory of knowledge, however, remains very obscure and very difficult to deal with. Let us see how these three problems arise.

(1) The logical problem has arisen through the suggestions of non-Euclidean geometry. Given a body of geometrical propositions, it is not difficult to find a minimum statement of the axioms from which this body of propositions can be deduced. It is also not difficult, by dropping or altering some of these axioms, to obtain a more general or a different geometry, having, from the point of view of pure mathematics, the same logical coherence and the same title to respect as the more familiar Euclidean geometry. The Euclidean geometry itself is true perhaps of actual space (though this is doubtful), but certainly of an infinite number of purely arithmetical systems, each of which, from the point of view of abstract logic, has an equal and indefeasible right to be called a Euclidean space. Thus space as an object of logical or mathematical study loses its uniqueness; not only are there many kinds of spaces, but there are an infinity of examples of each kind, though it is difficult to find any kind of which the space of physics may be an example, and it is impossible to find any kind of which the space of physics is certainly an example. As an illustration of one possible logical system of geometry we may consider all relations of three terms which are analogous in certain formal respects to the relation 'between' as it appears to be in actual space. A space is then defined by means of one such three-term relation. The points of the space are all the terms which have this relation to something or other, and their order in the space in question is determined by this relation. The points of one space are necessarily also points of other spaces, since there are necessarily other three-term relations having those same points for their field. The space in fact is not determined by the class of its points) but by the ordering three-term relation. When enough abstract logical properties of such relations have been enumerated to determine the resulting kind of geometry, say, for example, Euclidean geometry, it becomes unnecessary for the pure geometry in his abstract capacity to distinguish between the various relations which have all these properties. He considers the whole class of such relations, not any single one among them. Thus in studying a given kind of geometry the pure mathematician is studying a certain class of relations defined by means of certain abstract logical properties which take the place of what used to be called axioms. The nature of geometrical reasoning therefore is purely deductive and purely logical; if any special epistemological peculiarities are to be found in geometry, it must not be in the reasoning, but in our knowledge concerning the axioms in some given space.

(2) The physical problem of space is both more interesting and more difficult than the logical problem. The physical problem may be stated as follows: to find in the physical world, or to construct from physical materials, a space of one of the kinds enumerated by the logical treatment of geometry. This problem derives its difficulty from the attempt to accommodate to the roughness and vagueness of the real world some system possessing the logical clearness and exactitude of pure mathematics. That this can be done with a certain degree of approximation is fairly evident. If I see three people A, B, and C sitting in a row, I become aware of the fact which may be expressed by saying that B is between A and C rather than that A is between B and C, or C is between A and B. This relation of 'between' which is thus perceived to hold has some of the abstract logical properties of those three-term relations which, we saw, give rise to a geometry, but its properties fail to be exact, and are not, as empirically given, amenable to the kind of treatment at which geometry aims. In abstract geometry we deal with points, straight lines, and planes; but the three people A, B, and C whom I see sitting in a row are not exactly points, nor is the row exactly a straight line. Nevertheless physics, which formally assumes a space containing points, straight lines, and planes, is found empirically to give results applicable to the sensible world. It must therefore be possible to find an interpretation of the points, straight lines, and planes of physics in terms of physical data, or at any rate m terms of data together with such hypothetical additions as seem least open to question. Since all data suffer from a lack of mathematical precision through being of a certain size and somewhat vague in outline, it is plain that if such a notion as that of a point is to find any application to empirical material, the point must be neither a datum nor a hypothetical addition to data, but a construction by means of data with their hypothetical additions. It is obvious that any hypothetical filling out of data is less dubious and unsatisfactory when the additions are closely analogous to data than when they are of a radically different sort. To assume, for example, that objects which we see continue, after we have turned away our eyes, to be more or less analogous to what they were while we were looking, is a less violent assumption than to assume that such objects are composed of an infinite number of mathematical points. Hence in the physical

study of the geometry of physical space, Points must not be assumed *ab initio* as they are in the logical treatment of geometry, but must be constructed as systems composed of data and hypothetical analogues of data. We are thus led naturally to define a physical point as a certain class of those objects which are the ultimate constituents of the physical world. It will be the class of all those objects which, as one would naturally say, contain the point. To secure a definition giving this result, without previously assuming that physical objects are composed of points, is an agreeable problem in mathematical logic. The solution of this problem and the perception of its importance are due to my friend Dr. Whitehead. The oddity of regarding a point as a class of physical entities wears off with familiarity, and ought in any case not to be felt by those who maintain, as practically every one does, that points are mathematical fictions. The word 'fiction' is used glibly in such connexions by many men who seem not to feel the necessity of explaining how it can come about that a fiction can be so useful in the study of the actual world as the points of mathematical physics have been found to be. By our definition, which regards a point as a class of physical objects, it is explained both how the use of points can lead to important physical results, and how we can nevertheless avoid the assumption that points are themselves entities in the physical world.

Many of the mathematically convenient properties of abstract logical spaces cannot be either known to belong or known not to belong to the space of physics. Such are all the properties connected with continuity. For to know that actual space has these properties would require an infinite exactness of sense-perception. If actual space is continuous, there are nevertheless many possible non-continuous spaces which will be empirically indistinguishable from it; and, conversely, actual space may be non-continuous and yet empirically indistinguishable from a possible continuous space. Continuity, therefore, though obtainable in the a *priori* region of arithmetic, is not with certainty obtainable in the space or time of the physical world: whether these are continuous or not would seem to be a question not only unanswered but for ever unanswerable. From the point of view of philosophy, however, the discovery that a question is unanswerable is as complete an answer as any that could possibly be obtained. And from the point of view of physics, where no empirical means of distinction can be found, there can be no empirical objection to the mathematically simplest assumption, which is that of continuity.

The subject of the physical theory of space is a very large one, hitherto little explored. It is associated with a similar theory of time, and both have been forced upon the attention of philosophically minded physicists by the discussions which have raged concerning the theory of relativity.

(3) The problem with which Kant is concerned in the Transcendental Aesthetic is primarily the epistemological problem: 'How do we come to have knowledge of geometry a *priori*?' By the distinction between the logical and physical problems of geometry, the bearing and scope of this question are greatly altered. Our knowledge of pure geometry is a *priori* but is wholly logical. Our knowledge of physical geometry is synthetic, but is not a *priori* Our knowledge of pure geometry is hypothetical, and does not enable us to assert, for example, that the axiom of parallels is true in the physical world. Our knowledge of physical geometry, while it does enable us to assert that this axiom is approximately verified, does not, owing to the inevitable inexactitude of observation, enable us to assert that it is verified exactly. Thus, with the separation which we have made between pure geometry and the geometry of physics, the Kantian problem collapses. To the question, 'How is synthetic a *priori* knowledge possible?' we can now reply, at any rate so far as geometry is concerned, 'It is not possible,' if 'synthetic' means 'not deducible from logic alone.' Our knowledge of geometry, like the rest of our knowledge, is derived partly from logic, partly from sense, and the peculiar position which in Kant's day geometry appeared to occupy is seen now to be a delusion. There are still some philosophers, it is true, who maintain that our knowledge that the axiom of parallels, for example, is true of actual space, is not to be accounted for empirically, but is as Kant maintained derived from an a *priori* intuition. This position is not logically refutable, but I think it loses all plausibility as soon as we realize how complicated and derivative is the notion of physical space. As we have seen, the application of geometry to the physical world in no way demands that there should really be points and straight lines among physical entities. The principle of economy, therefore, demands that we should abstain from assuming the existence of points and straight lines. As soon, however, as we accept the view that points and straight lines are complicated constructions by means of classes of physical entities, the hypothesis that we have an a priori intuition enabling us to know what happens to straight lines when they are produced indefinitely becomes extremely strained and harsh; nor do I think that such an hypothesis would ever have arisen in the mind of a philosopher who had grasped the nature of physical space. Kant, under the influence of Newton, adopted, though with some vacillation, the hypothesis of absolute space, and this hypothesis, though logically unobjectionable, is removed by Occam's razor, since absolute space is an unnecessary entity in the explanation of the physical world. Although, therefore, we cannot refute the Kantian theory of an *a priori* intuition, we can remove its grounds one by one through an analysis of the problem. Thus, here as in many other philosophical questions, the analytic method, while not capable of arriving at a demonstrative result, is nevertheless capable of showing that all the positive grounds in favour of a certain theory are fallacious and that a less unnatural theory is capable of accounting for the facts.

Another question by which the capacity of the analytic method can be shown is the question of realism. Both those who advocate and those who combat realism seem to me to be far from clear as to he nature of the problem which they are discussing. If we ask: 'Are our objects of perception *real* and are they *independent* of the percipient?' it must be supposed that we attach some meaning to the words 'real' and 'independent', and yet, if either side in the controversy of realism is asked to define these two words, their answer is pretty sure to embody confusions such as logical analysis will reveal.

Let us begin with the word 'real'. There certainly are objects of perception, and therefore, if the question whether these objects are real is to be a substantial question, there must be in the world two sorts of objects, namely, the real and the unreal, and yet the unreal is supposed to be essentially what there is not. The question what properties must belong to an object in order to make it real is one to which an adequate answer is seldom if ever forthcoming. There is of course the Hegelian answer, that the real is the self-consistent and that nothing is self-consistent except the whole; but this answer, true or false, is not relevant in our present discussion, which moves on a lower plane and is concerned with the status of objects of perception among other objects of equal fragmentariness. Objects of perception are contrasted, in the discussions concerning realism, rather with psychical states on the one hand and matter on the other hand than with the all-inclusive whole of things. The question we have therefore to consider is the question as to what can be meant by assigning 'reality' to some but not all of the entities that make up the world. Two elements, I think, make up what is felt rather than thought when the word 'reality' is used in this sense. A thing is real if it persists at times when it is not perceived; or again, a thing is real when it is correlated with other things in a way which experience has led us to expect. It will be seen that reality in either of these senses is by no means necessary to a thing, and that in fact there might be a whole world in which nothing was real in either of these senses. It might turn out that the objects of perception failed of reality in one or both of these respects, without its being in any way deducible that they are not parts of the external world with which physics deals. Similar remarks will apply to the word 'independent'. Most of the associations of this word are bound up with ideas as to causation which it is not now possible to maintain. A is independent of B when B is not an indispensable part of the *cause* of A. But when it is recognized that causation is nothing more than correlation, and that there are correlations of simultaneity as well as of succession, it becomes evident that there is no uniqueness in a series of casual antecedents of a given event, but that, at any point where there is a correlation of simultaneity, we can pass from one line of antecedents to another in order to obtain a new series of causal antecedents. It will be necessary to specify the causal law according to which the antecedents are to be considered. I received a letter the other day from a correspondent who had been puzzled by various philosophical questions. After enumerating them he says: "These questions led me from Bonn to Strassburg, where I found Professor Simmel.' Now, it would be absurd to deny that these questions caused his body to move from Bonn to Strassburg, and yet it must be supposed that a set of purely mechanical antecedents could also be found which would account for this transfer of matter from one place to another. Owing to this plurality of causal series antecedent to a given event, the notion of *the* cause becomes indefinite, and the question of independence becomes correspondingly ambiguous. Thus, instead of asking simply whether A is independent of B, we ought to ask whether there is a series determined by such and such causal laws leading from B to A. This point is important in connexion with the particular question of objects of perception. It may be that no objects quite like those which we perceive ever exist unperceived; in this case there will be a causal law according to which objects of perception are not independent of being perceived. But even if this be the case, it may nevertheless also happen that there are purely physical causal laws determining the occurrence of objects which are perceived by means of other objects which perhaps are not perceived. In that case, in regard to such causal laws objects of perception will be independent of being perceived. Thus the question whether objects of perception are independent of being perceived is, as it stands, indeterminate, and the answer will be yes or no according to the method adopted of making it determinate. I believe that this confusion has borne a very large part in prolonging the controversies on this subject, which might well have seemed capable of remaining for ever undecided. The view which I should wish to advocate is that objects of perception do not persist unchanged at times when they are not perceived, although probably objects more or less resembling them do exist at such times; that objects of perception are part, and the only empirically knowable part, of the actual subject-matter of physics, and are themselves properly to be called physical; that purely physical laws exist determining the character and duration of objects of perception without any reference to the fact that they are perceived; and that in the establishment of such laws the propositions of physics do not presuppose any propositions of psychology or even the existence of mind. I do not know whether realists would recognize such a view as realism. All that I should claim for it is, that it avoids difficulties which seem to me to beset both realism and idealism as hitherto advocated, and that it avoids the appeal which they have made to ideas which logical analysis shows to be ambiguous. A further defence and elaboration of the positions which I advocate, but for which time is lacking now, will be found indicated in my book on *Our Knowledge of the External World*.[5]

The adoption of scientific method in philosophy, if I am not mistaken, compels us to abandon the hope of solving many of the more ambitious and humanly interesting problems of traditional philosophy. Some of these it

---

[5] Open Court Company, 1914

relegates, though with little expectation of a successful solution, to special sciences, others it shows to be such as our capacities are essentially incapable of solving. But there remain a large number of the recognized problems of philosophy in regard to which the method advocated gives all those advantages of division into distinct questions, of tentative, partial, and progressive advance, and of appeal to principles with which, independently of temperament, all competent students must agree. The failure of philosophy hitherto has been due in the main to haste and ambition: patience and modesty, here as in other sciences, will open the road to solid and durable progress.

LINGUISTIC CONTRIBUTIONS TO THE STUDY OF MIND ------- *Past*

In these lectures, I would like to focus attention on the question, What contribution can the study of language make to our understanding of human nature? In one or another manifestation, this question threads its way through modern Western thought. In an age that was less self-conscious and less compartmentalized than ours, the nature of language, the respects in which language mirrors human mental processes or shapes the flow and character of thought -- these were topics for study and speculation by scholars and gifted amateurs with a wide variety of interests, points of view, and intellectual backgrounds. And in the nineteenth and twentieth centuries, as linguistics, philosophy, and psychology have uneasily tried to go their separate ways, the classical problems of language and mind have inevitably reappeared and have served to link these diverging fields and to give direction and significance to their efforts. There have been signs in the past decade that the rather artificial separation of disciplines may be coming to an end. It is no longer a point of honor for each to demonstrate its absolute independence of the others, and new interests have emerged that permit the classical problems to be formulated in novel and occasionally suggestive ways -- for example, in terms of the new perspectives provided by cybernetics and the communication sciences, and against the background of developments in comparative and physiological psychology that challenge long-standing convictions and free the scientific imagination from certain shackles that had become so familiar a part of our intellectual environment as to be almost beyond awareness. All of this is highly encouraging. I think there is more of a healthy ferment in cognitive psychology -- and in the particular branch of cognitive psychology known as linguistics -- than there has been for many years. And one of the most encouraging signs is that skepticism with regard to the orthodoxies of the recent past is coupled with an awareness of the temptations and the dangers of premature orthodoxy, an awareness that, if it can persist, may prevent the rise of new and stultifying dogma.

It is easy to be misled in an assessment of the current scene; nevertheless, it seems to me that the decline of dogmatism and the accompanying search for new approaches to old and often still intractable problems are quite unmistakable, not only in linguistics but in all of the disciplines concerned with the study of mind. I remember quite clearly my own feeling of uneasiness as a student at the fact that, so it seemed, the basic problems of the field were solved, and that what remained was to sharpen and improve techniques of linguistic analysis that were reasonably well understood and to apply them to a wider range of linguistic materials. In the postwar years, this was a dominant attitude in most active centers of research. I recall being told by a distinguished anthropological linguist, in 1953, that he had no intention of working through a vast collection of materials that he had assembled because within a few years it would surely be possible to program a computer to construct a grammar from a large corpus of data by the use of techniques that were already fairly well formalized. At the time, this did not seem an unreasonable attitude, though the prospect was saddening for anyone who felt, or at least hoped, that the resources of human intelligence were somewhat deeper than these procedures and techniques might reveal. Correspondingly, there was a striking decline in studies of linguistic method in the early 1950's as the most active theoretical minds turned to the problem of how an essentially closed body of technique could be applied to some new domain -- say, to analysis of connected discourse, or to other cultural phenomena beyond language. I arrived at Harvard as a graduate student shortly after B. F. Skinner had delivered his William James Lectures, later to be published in his book *Verbal Behavior*. Among those active in research in the philosophy or psychology of language, there was then little doubt that although details were missing, and although matters could not really be quite that simple, nevertheless a behavioristic framework of the sort Skinner had outlined would prove quite adequate to accommodate the full range of language use. There was now little reason to question the conviction of Leonard Bloomfield, Bertrand Russell, and positivistic linguists, psychologists, and philosophers in general that the framework of stimulus-response psychology would soon be extended to the point where it would provide a satisfying explanation for the most mysterious of human abilities. The most radical souls felt that perhaps, in order to do full justice to these abilities, one must postulate little s's and r's inside the brain alongside the capital S's and R's that were open to immediate inspection, but this extension was not inconsistent with the general picture.

Critical voices, even those that commanded considerable prestige, were simply unheard. For example, Karl Lashley gave a brilliant critique of the prevailing framework of ideas in 1948, arguing that underlying language use -- and all organized behavior -- there must be abstract mechanisms of some sort that are not analyzable in terms of association and that could not have been developed by any such simple means. But his arguments and proposals, though sound and perceptive, had absolutely no effect on the development of the field and went by unnoticed even at his own university (Harvard), then the leading center of psycholinguistic research. Ten years later Lashley's contribution began to be appreciated, but only after his insights had been independently achieved in another context.

The technological advances of the 1940's simply reinforced the general euphoria. Computers were on the horizon, and their imminent availability reinforced the belief that it would suffice to gain a theoretical understanding of only the simplest and most superficially obvious of phenomena -- everything else would merely prove to be "more of the same," an apparent complexity that would be disentangled by the electronic marvels. The sound spectrograph, developed during the war, offered similar promise for the physical analysis of speech sounds. The interdisciplinary conferences on speech analysis of the early 1950's make interesting reading today. There were few so benighted as to question the possibility, in fact the immediacy, of a final solution to the problem of converting speech into writing by available engineering technique. And just a few years later, it was jubilantly discovered that machine translation and automatic abstracting were also just around the corner. For those who sought a more mathematical formulation of the basic processes, there was the newly developed mathematical theory of communication, which, it was widely believed in the early 1950's, had provided a fundamental concept -- the concept of "information" -- that would unify the social and behavioral sciences and permit the development of a solid and satisfactory mathematical theory of human behavior on a probabilistic base. At about the same time, the theory of automata developed as an independent study, making use of closely related mathematical notions. And it was linked at once, and quite properly, to earlier explorations of the theory of neural nets. There were those -- John von Neumann, for example -- who felt that the entire development was dubious and shaky at best, and probably quite misconceived, but such qualms did not go far to dispel the feeling that mathematics, technology, and behavioristic linguistics and psychology were converging on a point of view that was very simple, very clear, and fully adequate to provide a basic understanding of what tradition had left shrouded in mystery.

In the United States at least, there is little trace today of the illusions of the early postwar years. If we consider the current status of structural linguistic methodology, stimulus-response psycholinguistics (whether or not extended to "mediation theory"), or probabilistic or automata-theoretic models for language use, we find that in each case a parallel development has taken place: A careful analysis has shown that insofar as the system of concepts and principles that was advanced can be made precise, it can be demonstrated to be inadequate in a fundamental way. The kinds of structures that are realizable in terms of these theories are simply not those that must be postulated to underlie the use of language, if empirical conditions of adequacy are to be satisfied. What is more, the character of the failure and inadequacy is such as to give little reason to believe that these approaches are on the right track. That is, in each case it has been argued -- quite persuasively, in my opinion -- that the approach is not only inadequate but misguided in basic and important ways. It has, I believe, become quite clear that if we are ever to understand how language is used or acquired, then we must abstract for separate and independent study a cognitive system, a system of knowledge and belief, that develops in early childhood and that interacts with many other factors to determine the kinds of behavior that we observe; to introduce a technical term, we must isolate and study the system of linguistic competence that underlies behavior but that is not realized in any direct or simple way in behavior. And this system of linguistic competence is qualitatively different from anything that can be described in terms of the taxonomic methods of structural linguistics, the concepts of S-R psychology, or the notions developed within the mathematical theory of communication or the theory of simple automata. The theories and models that were developed to describe simple and immediately given phenomena cannot incorporate the real system of linguistic competence; "extrapolation" for simple descriptions cannot approach the reality of linguistic competence; mental structures are not simply "more of the same" but are qualitatively different from the complex networks and structures that can be developed by elaboration of the concepts that seemed so promising to many scientists just a few years ago. What is involved is not a matter of degree of complexity but rather a quality of complexity. Correspondingly, there is no reason to expect that the available technology can provide significant insight or understanding or useful achievements; it has noticeably failed to do so, and, in fact, an appreciable investment of time, energy, and money in the use of computers for linguistic research -- appreciable by the standards of a small field like linguistics -- has not provided any significant advance in our understanding of the use or nature of language. These judgments are harsh, but I think they are defensible. They are, furthermore, hardly debated by active linguistic or psycholinguistic researchers.

At the same time there have been significant advances, I believe, in our understanding of the nature of linguistic competence and some of the ways in which it is put to use, but these advances, such as they are, have proceeded from assumptions very different from those that were so enthusiastically put forth in the period I have been discussing. What is more, these advances have not narrowed the gap between what is known and what can be seen to lie beyond the scope of present understanding and technique; rather, each advance has made it clear that these intellectual horizons are far more remote than was heretofore imagined. Finally, it has become fairly clear, it seems to me, that the assumptions and approaches that appear to be productive today have a distinctly traditional flavor to them; in general, a much despised tradition has been largely revitalized in recent years and its contributions given some serious and, I believe, well-deserved attention. From the recognition of these facts flows the general and quite healthy attitude of skepticism that I spoke of earlier.

In short, it seems to me quite appropriate, at this moment in the development of linguistics and psychology in general, to turn again to classical questions and to ask what new insights have been achieved that bear on them, and how the classical issues may provide direction for contemporary research and study.

When we turn to the history of study and speculation concerning the nature of mind and, more specifically, the nature of human language, our attention quite naturally comes to focus on the seventeenth century, "the century of genius," in which the foundations of modern science were firmly established and the problems that still confound us were formulated with remarkable clarity and perspicuity. There are many far from superficial respects in which the intellectual climate of today resembles that of seventeenth-century Western Europe. One, particularly crucial in the present context, is the very great interest in the potentialities and capacities of automata, a problem that intrigued the seventeenth-century mind as fully as it does our own. I mentioned above that there is a slowly dawning realization that a significant gap -- more accurately, a yawning chasm -- separates the system of concepts of which we have a fairly clear grasp, on the one hand, and the nature of human intelligence, on the other. A similar realization lies at the base of Cartesian philosophy. Descartes also arrived, quite early in his investigations, at the conclusion that the study of mind faces us with a problem of quality of complexity, not merely degree of complexity. He felt that he had demonstrated that understanding and will, the two fundamental properties of the human mind, involved capacities and principles that are not realizable by even the most complex of automata.

It is particularly interesting to trace the development of this argument in the works of the minor and now quite forgotten Cartesian philosophers, like Cordemoy, who wrote a fascinating treatise extending Descartes' few remarks about language, or La Forge, who produced a long and detailed *Traite' de l'esprit de l'homme* expressing, so he claimed with some reason, what Descartes would likely have said about this subject had he lived to extend his theory of man beyond physiology. One may question the details of this argument, and one can show how it was impeded and distorted by certain remnants of scholastic doctrine -- the framework of substance and mode, for example. But the general structure of the argument is not unreasonable; it is, in fact, rather analogous to the argument against the framework of ideas of the early postwar years, which I mentioned at the outset of this lecture. The Cartesians tried to show that when the theory of corporeal body is sharpened and clarified and extended to its limits, it is still incapable of accounting for facts that are obvious to introspection and that are also confirmed by our observation of the actions of other humans. In particular, it cannot account for the normal use of human language, just as it cannot explain the basic properties of thought. Consequently, it becomes necessary to invoke an entirely new principle -- in Cartesian terms, to postulate a second substance whose essence is thought, alongside of body, with its essential properties of extension and motion. This new principle has a "creative aspect," which is evidenced most clearly in what we may refer to as "the creative aspect of language use," the distinctively human ability to express new thoughts and to understand entirely new expressions of thought, within the framework of an "instituted language," a language that is a cultural product subject to laws and principles partially unique to it and partially reflections of general properties of mind. These laws and principles, it is maintained, are not formulable in terms of even the most elaborate extension of the concepts proper to the analysis of behavior and interaction of physical bodies, and they are not realizable by even the most complex automaton. In fact, Descartes argued that the only sure indication that another body possesses a human mind, that it is not a mere automaton, is its ability to use language in the normal way; and he argued that this ability cannot be detected in an animal or an automaton which, in other respects, shows signs of apparent intelligence exceeding those of a human, even though such an organism or machine might be as fully endowed as a human with the physiological organs necessary to produce speech.

I will return to this argument and the ways in which it was developed. But I think it is important to stress that, with all its gaps and deficiencies, it is an argument that must be taken seriously. There is nothing at all absurd in the conclusion. It seems to me quite possible that at that particular moment in the development of Western thought there was the possibility for the birth of a science of psychology of a sort that still does not exist, a psychology that begins with the problem of characterizing various systems of human knowledge and belief, the concepts in terms of which they are organized and the principles that underlie them, and that only then turns to the study of how these systems might have developed through some combination of innate structure and organism-environment interaction. Such a psychology would contrast rather sharply with the approach to human intelligence that begins by postulating, on a priori grounds, certain specific mechanisms that, it is claimed, *must* be those underlying the acquisition of all knowledge and belief. The distinction is one to which I will return in a subsequent lecture. For the moment, I want merely to stress the reasonableness of the rejected alternative and, what is more, its consistency with the approach that proved so successful in the seventeenth-century revolution in physics.

There are methodological parallels that have perhaps been inadequately appreciated between the Cartesian postulation of a substance whose essence was thought and the post-Newtonian acceptance of a principle of attraction as an innate property of the ultimate corpuscles of matter, an active principle that governs the motions of bodies. Perhaps the most far-reaching contribution of Cartesian philosophy to modern thought was its rejection of the scholastic notion of substantial forms and real qualities, of all those "little images fluttering through the air" to which Descartes referred with derision; With the exorcism of these occult qualities, the stage was set for the rise of a physics of matter in motion and a psychology that explored the properties of mind. But Newton argued that Descartes' mechanical physics wouldn't work -- the second book of the *Principia* is largely devoted to this demonstration -- and that it is necessary to postulate a new force to account for the motion of bodies. The postulate of an attractive force acting at a distance was inconsistent with the clear and distinct ideas of common sense and could not be tolerated by an orthodox Cartesian -- such a force was merely another occult quality. Newton quite agreed, and he attempted repeatedly to find a mechanical explanation of the cause of gravity. He rejected the view that gravity is "essential and inherent to matter" and maintained that "to tell us that every species of things is endowed with an occult specific property (such as gravity) by which it acts and produces manifest effects, is to tell us nothing." Some historians of science have suggested that Newton hoped, like Descartes, to write a Principles of Philosophy but that his failure to explain the cause of gravity on mechanical grounds restricted him to a *Mathematical Principles of Natural Philosophy.* Thus, to the common sense of Newton as well as the Cartesians, physics was still not adequately grounded, because it postulated a mystical force capable of action at a distance. Similarly, Descartes' postulation of mind as an explanatory principle was unacceptable to the empiricist temper. But the astonishing success of mathematical physics carried the day against these common-sense objections, and the prestige of the new physics was so high that the speculative psychology of the Enlightenment took for granted the necessity of working within the Newtonian framework, rather than on the Newtonian analogy -- a very different matter. The occult force of gravity was accepted as an obvious element of the physical world, requiring no explanation, and it became inconceivable that one might have to postulate entirely new principles of functioning and organization outside the framework of what soon became the new "common sense." Partly for this reason, the search for an analogous scientific psychology that would explore the principles of mind, whatever they might be, was not undertaken with the thoroughness that was then, as now, quite possible.

    I do not want to overlook a fundamental distinction between the postulation of gravity and the postulation of a *res cogitans*, namely the enormous disparity in the power of the explanatory theories that were developed. Nevertheless, I think it is instructive to note that the reasons for the dissatisfaction of Newton, Leibnitz, and the orthodox Cartesians with the new physics are strikingly similar to the grounds on which a dualistic rationalist psychology was soon to be rejected. I think it is correct to say that the study of properties and organization of mind was prematurely abandoned, in part on quite spurious grounds, and also to point out that there is a certain irony in the common view that its abandonment was caused by the gradual spread of a more general "scientific" attitude.

I have tried to call attention to some similarities between the intellectual climate of the seventeenth century and that of today. It is illuminating, I think, to trace in somewhat greater detail the specific course of development of linguistic theory during the modern period, in the contest of the study of mind and of behavior in general.[1]

A good place to begin is with the writings of the Spanish physician Juan Huarte, who in the late sixteenth century published a widely translated study on the nature of human intelligence. In the course of his investigations, Huarte came to wonder at the fact that the word for "intelligence," ingenio, seems to have the same Latin root as various words meaning "engender" or "generate." This, he argued, gives a clue to the nature of mind. Thus, "One may discern two generative powers in man, one common with the beasts and the plants, and the other participating substance. Wit (Ingenjo) is a generative power. The understanding is a generative faculty." Huarte's etymology is actually not very good; the insight, however, is quite substantial.

Huarte goes on to distinguish three levels of intelligence. The lowest of these is the "docile wit," which satisfies the maxim that he, along with Leibnitz and many others, wrongly attributes to Aristotle, namely that there is nothing in the mind that is not simply transmitted to it by the senses. The next higher level, normal human intelligence, goes well beyond the empiricist limitation: It is able to "engender within itself, by its own power, the principles on which knowledge rests." Normal human minds are such that "assisted by the subject alone, without the help of anybody, they will produce a thousand conceits they never heard spoke of. . . inventing and saying such things as they never heard from their masters, nor any mouth." Thus, normal human intelligence is capable of acquiring knowledge through its own internal resources, perhaps making use of the data of sense but going on to construct a cognitive system in terms of concepts and principles that are developed on independent grounds; and it is capable of generating new thoughts and of finding appropriate and novel ways of expressing them, in ways that entirely transcend any training or experience.

Huarte postulates a third kind of wit, "by means of which some, without art or study, speak such subtle and surprising things, yet true, that were never before seen, heard, or writ, no, nor ever so much as thought of." The reference here is to true creativity, an exercise of the creative imagination in ways that go beyond normal intelligence and may, he felt, involve "a mixture of madness."

Huarte maintains that the distinction between docile wit, which meets the empiricist maxim, and normal intelligence, with its full generative, capacities, is the distinction between beast and man. As a physician, Huarte was much

---

[1] For additional details and discussion, see my *Cartesian Linguistics* (New York: Harper & Row, 1966) and the references cited there.

interested in pathology. In particular, he notes that the most severe disability of wit that can afflict a human is a restriction to the lowest of the three levels, to the docile wit that conforms to empiricist principles. This disability, says Huarte, "resembles that of Eunuchs, incapable of generation." Under these sad circumstances, in which the intelligence can only receive stimuli transmitted by sense and associate them with one another, true education is of course impossible, since the ideas and principles that permit the growth of knowledge and understanding are lacking. In this case, then, "neither the lash of the rod, nor cries, nor method, nor examples, nor time, nor experience, nor anything in nature can sufficiently excite him to bring forth anything."

Huarte's framework is useful for discussing "psychological theory" in the ensuing period. Typical of later thought is his reference to use of language as an index of human intelligence, of what distinguishes man from animals, and, specifically, his emphasis on the creative capacity of normal intelligence. These concerns dominated rationalist psychology and linguistics. With the rise of romanticism, attention shifted to the third type of wit, to true creativity, although the rationalist assumption that normal human intelligence is uniquely free and creative and beyond the bounds of mechanical explanation was not abandoned and played an important role in the psychology of romanticism, and even in its social philosophy.

As I have already mentioned, the rationalist theory of language, which was to prove extremely rich in insight and achievement, developed in part out of a concern with the problem of other minds. A fair amount of effort was devoted to a consideration of the ability of animals to follow spoken commands, to express their emotional states, to communicate with one another, and even apparently to cooperate for a common goal; all of this, it was argued, could be accounted for on "mechanical grounds," as this notion was then understood -- that is, through the functioning of physiological mechanisms in terms of which one could formulate the properties of reflexes, conditioning and reinforcement, association, and so on. Animals do not lack appropriate organs of communication, nor are they simply lower along some scale of "general intelligence."

In fact, as Descartes himself quite correctly observed, language is a species-specific human possession, and even at low levels of intelligence, at pathological levels, we find a command of language that is totally unattainable by an ape that may, in other respects, surpass a human imbecile in problem-solving ability and other adaptive behavior. I will return later to the status of this observation, in the light of what is now known about animal communication. There is a basic element lacking in animals, Descartes argued, as it is lacking in even the most complex automaton that develops its "intellectual structures" completely in terms of conditioning and association -- namely Huarte's second type of wit, the generative ability that is revealed in the normal human use of language as a free instrument of thought. If by experiment we convince ourselves that another organism gives evidence of the normal, creative use of language, we suppose that it, like us, has a mind and that what it does lies beyond the bounds of mechanical explanation, outside the framework of stimulus-response psychology of the time, which in relevant essentials is not significantly different from that of today, though it falls in sharpness of technique and scope and reliability of information.

It should not be thought, incidentally, that the only Cartesian arguments for the beast-machine hypothesis were those derived from the apparent inability of animals to manifest the creative aspect of language use. There were also many others -- for example, the natural fear of population explosion in the domains of the spirit if every gnat had a soul. Or the argument of Cardinal Melchior de Polignac, who argued that the beast-machine hypothesis followed from the assumption of the goodness of God, since, as he pointed out, one can see "how much more humane is doctrine that animals suffer no pain."[2] Or there is the argument of Lorns Racine, son of the dramatist, who was struck by the following in-sight: "If beasts had souls and were capable of feelings, would they show themselves insensible to the affront and injustice done them by Descartes? Would they not rather have risen up in wrath against the leader and the sect which so degraded them?" One should add, I suppose, that Louis Racine was regarded by his contemporaries as the living proof that a brilliant father could not have a brilliant son. But the fact is that the discussion of the existence of other minds, and, in contrast, the mechanical nature of animals, continually returned to the creative aspect of language use, to the claim that -- as formulated by another minor seventeenth-century figure -- "if beasts reasoned, they would be capable of true speech with its infinite variety."

It is important to understand just what properties of language were most striking to Descartes and his followers. The discussion of what I have been calling "the creative aspect of language use" turns on three important observations. The first is that the normal use of language is innovative, in the sense that much of what we say in the course of normal language use is entirely new, not a repetition of anything that we have heard before and not even similar in pattern -- in any useful sense of the terms "similar" and "pattern" -- to sentences or discourse that we have heard in the past. This is a truism, but an important one, often overlooked and not infrequently denied in the behaviorist period of linguistics to which I referred earlier, when it was almost universally claimed that a person's knowledge of language is representable as a stored set of patterns, overlearned through constant repetition and detailed training, with innovation being at most a matter of "analogy." The fact surely is, however, that

---

[2] These examples are taken from the excellent study by Leonora Cohen Rosenfield, From Beast-Machine to Man-Machine (New York: Oxford University Press, 1941). The quotes are her paraphrases of the original.

the number of sentences in one's native language that one will immediately understand with no feeling of difficulty or strangeness is astronomical; and that the number of patterns underlying our normal use of language and corresponding to meaningful and easily comprehensible sentences in our language is orders of magnitude greater than the number of seconds in a lifetime. It is in this sense that the normal use of language is innovative.

However, in the Cartesian view even animal behavior is potentially infinite in its variety, in the special sense in which the readings of a speedometer can be said, with an obvious idealization, to be potentially infinite in variety. That is, if animal behavior is controlled by external stimuli or internal states (the latter including those established by conditioning), then as the stimuli vary over an indefinite range, so may the behavior of the animal. But the normal use of language is not only innovative and potentially infinite in scope, but also free from the control of detectable stimuli, either external or internal. It is because of this freedom from stimulus control that language can serve as an instrument of thought and self-expression, as it does not only for the exceptionally gifted and talented, but also, in fact, for every normal human.

Still, the properties of being unbounded and free from stimulus control do not, in themselves, exceed the bounds of mechanical explanation. And Cartesian discussion of the limits of mechanical explanation therefore took note of a third property of the normal use of language, namely its coherence and its "appropriateness to the situation" -- which of course is an entirely different matter from control by external stimuli. Just what "appropriateness" and "coherence" may consist in we cannot say in any clear or definite way, but there is no doubt that these are meaningful concepts. We can distinguish normal use of language from the ravings of a maniac or the output of a computer with a random element.

Honesty forces us to admit that we are as far today as Descartes was three centuries ago from understanding just what enables a human to speak in a way that is innovative, free from stimulus control, and also appropriate and coherent. This is a serious problem that the psychologist must ultimately face and that cannot be talked out of existence by invoking "habit" or "conditioning" or "natural selection."

The Cartesian analysis of the problem of other minds, in terms of the creative aspect of language use and similar indications of the limits of mechanical explanation, was not entirely satisfying to contemporary opinion -- Baley's *Dictionary,* for example, cites the inability to give a satisfactory proof of the existence of other minds as the weakest element in the Cartesian philosophy -- and there was a long and intriguing series of discussions and polemics regarding the problems that Descartes raised. From the vantage point of several centuries, we can see that the debate was inconclusive. The properties of human thought and human language emphasized by the Cartesians are real enough; they were then, as they are now, beyond the bounds of any well-understood kind of physical explanation. Neither physics nor biology nor psychology gives us any clue as to how to deal with these matters.

As in the case of other intractable problems, it is tempting to try another approach, one that might show the problem to be misconceived, the result of some conceptual confusion. This is a line of argument that has been followed in contemporary philosophy, but, it seems to me, without success. It is clear that the Cartesians understood, as well as Gilbert Ryle and other contemporary critics understand, the difference between providing criteria for intelligent behavior, on the one hand, and providing an explanation for the possibility of such behavior, on the other; but, as distinct from Ryle, they were interested in the latter problem as well as the former. As scientists, they were not satisfied with the formulation of experimental tests that would show the behavior of another organism to be creative, in the special sense just outlined; they were also troubled, and quite rightly so, by the fact that the abilities indicated by such tests and observational criteria transcended the capacities of corporeal bodies as they understood them, just as they are beyond the scope of physical explanation as we understand it today. There is surely nothing illegitimate in an attempt to go beyond elaboration of observational tests and collection of evidence to the construction of some theoretical explanation for what is observed, and this just what was at stake in the Cartesian approach to the problem of mind. As La Forge and others insisted, it is necessary to go beyond what one can perceive or imagine" (in the technical, classical sense of this term) if one hopes to understand the nature of "l'esprit de l'homme," just as Newton did -- successfully -- in trying to understand the nature of planetary motion. On the other hand, the proposals of the Cartesians were themselves of no real substance; the phenomena in question are not explained satisfactorily by attributing them to an "active principle" called "mind," the properties of which are not developed in any coherent or comprehensive way.

It seems to me that the most hopeful approach today is to describe the phenomena of language and of mental activity as accurately as possible, to try to develop an abstract theoretical apparatus that will as far as possible account for these phenomena and reveal the principles of their organization and functioning, without attempting, for the present, to relate the postulated mental structures and processes to any physiological mechanisms or to interpret mental function in terms of "physical causes. We can only leave open for the future the question of how these abstract structures and processes are realized or accounted for in some concrete terms, conceivably in terms that are not within the range of physical processes as presently understood -- a conclusion that, if correct, should surprise no one.

This rationalist philosophy of language merged with various other independent developments in the seventeenth century, leading to the first really significant general theory of linguistic structure, namely the general point of view that came to be known as "philosophical" or "universal" grammar. Unfortunately, philosophical grammar is very poorly known today. There are few technical or scholarly studies, and these few are apologetic and disparaging. References to philosophical grammar in modern treatises on language are so distorted as to be quite worthless. Even a scholar with such high standards as Leonard Bloomfield gives an account of philosophical grammar in his major work, *Language*, that bears almost no resemblance to the original and attributes to this tradition views diametrically opposed to those that were most typical of it. For example, Bloomfield and many others describe philosophical grammar as based on a Latin model, as prescriptive, as showing no interest in the sounds of speech, as given to a confusion of speech with writing. All these charges are false, and it is important to dispel these myths to make possible an objective evaluation of what was actually accomplished.

It is particularly ironic that philosophical grammar should be accused of a Latin bias. In fact, it is significant that the original works -- the Port-Royal *Grammar* and *Logic*, in particular -- were written in French, the point being that they formed part of the movement to replace Latin by the vernacular. The fact is that Latin was regarded as an artificial and distorted language, one positively injurious to the exercise of the plain thinking and common-sense discourse by which the Cartesians set such store. The practitioners of philosophical grammar used such linguistic materials as were available to them; it is noteworthy that some of the topics that were studied with the greatest care and persistence for well over a century involved points of grammar that do not even have an analogue in Latin. A striking example is the so-called rule of Vaugelas, which involves the relation between indefinite articles and relative clauses in French. For a hundred and fifty years the rule of Vaugelas was the central issue debated in the controversy over the possibility of developing a "rational grammar," one which would go beyond description to achieve a rational explanation for phenomena.

No doubt it is a complete misunderstanding of the issue of rational explanation that leads to the charge of "prescriptivism" that is leveled, quite erroneously, against philosophical grammar. In fact, there is no issue of prescriptivism. It was well understood and frequently reiterated that the facts of usage are what they are, and that it is not the place of the grammarian to legislate. At stake was an entirely different matter, namely the problem of accounting for the facts of usage on the basis of explanatory hypotheses concerning the nature of language and, ultimately, the nature of human thought. Philosophical grammarians had little interest in the accumulation of data, except insofar as such data could be used as evidence bearing on deeper processes of great generality. The contrast, then, is not between descriptive and prescriptive grammar, but between description and explanation, between grammar as "natural history" and grammar as a kind of "natural philosophy" or, in modern terms, "natural science." A largely irrational objection to explanatory theories as such has made it difficult for modern linguistics to appreciate what was actually at stake in these developments and has led to a confusion of philosophical grammar with the effort to teach better manners to a rising middle class.

The whole matter is not without interest. I mentioned earlier that there are striking similarities between the seventeenth-century climate of opinion and that of contemporary cognitive psychology and linguistics. One point of similarity has to do with precisely this matter of explanatory theory. Philosophical grammar, very much like current generative grammar, developed in self-conscious opposition to a descriptive tradition that interpreted the task of the grammarian to be merely that of recording and organizing the data of usage -- a kind of natural history. It maintained -- quite correctly, I believe -- that such a restriction was debilitating and unnecessary and that, whatever justification it may have, it has nothing to do with the method of science -- which is typically concerned with data not for itself but as evidence for deeper, hidden organizing principles, principles that cannot be detected "in the phenomena" nor derived from them by taxonomic data-processing operations, any more than the principles of celestial mechanics could have been developed in conformity with such strictures.

Contemporary scholarship is not in a position to give a definitive assessment of the achievements of philosophical grammar. The groundwork has not been laid for such an assessment, the original work is all but unknown in itself, and much of it is almost unobtainable. For example, I have been unable to locate a single copy, in the United States, of the only critical edition of the Port-Royal *Grammar*, produced over a century ago; and although the French original is now once again available,[3] the one English translation of this important work is apparently to be found only in the British Museum. It is a pity that this work should have been so totally disregarded, since what little is known about it is intriguing and quite illuminating.

This is not the place to attempt a preliminary assessment of this work or even to sketch its major outlines as they now appear, on the basis of present, quite inadequate knowledge. However, I do want to mention at least a few of the persistent themes. It seems that one of the innovations of the Port-Royal *Grammar* of 1660 -- the work that initiated the tradition of philosophical grammar -- was its recognition of the importance of the notion of the phrase as a grammatical unit. Earlier grammar had been largely a grammar of word classes and inflections. In the Cartesian theory of Port-Royal, a phrase corresponds to a complex idea and a sentence is subdivided into consecutive phrases, which are further subdivided into phrases, and so on, until the level of the word is reached. In this way we derive what might be called the "surface structure" of the sentence in question. To use what became a standard example, the sentence "Invisible God created the visible world" contains the subject "invisible God" and the

---

[3] Menston, England: Scolar Press Limited, 1967.

predicate "created the visible world," the latter contains the complex idea "the visible world" and the verb "created," and so on. But it is interesting that although the Port-Royal *Grammar* is apparently the first to rely in a fairly systematic way on analysis into surface structure, it also recognized the inadequacy of such analysis. According to the Port-Royal theory, surface structure corresponds only to sound -- to the corporeal aspect of language; but when the signal is produced, with its surface structure, there takes place a corresponding mental analysis into what we may call the deep structure, a formal structure that relates directly not to the sound but to the meaning. In the example just given, "Invisible God created the visible world," the deep structure consists of a system of three propositions, "that God is invisible," "that he created the world," "that the world is visible." The propositions that interrelate to form the deep structure are not, of course, asserted when the sentence is used to make a statement; if I say that a wise man is honest, I am not asserting that men are wise or honest, even though in the Port-Royal theory the propositions "a man is wise" and "a man is honest" enter into the deep structure. Rather, these propositions enter into the complex ideas that are present to the mind, though rarely articulated in the signal, when the sentence is uttered.

The deep structure is related to the surface structure by certain mental operations -- in modern terminology, by grammatical transformations. Each language can be regarded as a particular relation between sound and meaning. Following the Port-Royal theory to its logical conclusions, then, the grammar of a language must contain a system of rules that characterizes deep and surface structures and the transformational relation between them, and -- if it is to accommodate the creative aspect of language use -- that does so over an infinite domain of paired deep and surface structures. To use the terminology Wilhelm von Humboldt used in the 1830's, the speaker makes infinite use of finite means. His grammar must, then, contain a finite system of rules that generates infinitely many deep and surface structures, appropriately related. It must also contain rules that relate these abstract structures to certain representations of sound and meaning -- representations that, presumably, are constituted of elements that belong to universal phonetics and universal semantics, respectively. In essence, this is the concept of grammatical structure as it is being developed and elaborated today. Its roots are clearly to be found in the classical tradition that I am now discussing, and the basic concepts were explored with some success in this period.

The theory of deep and surface structure seems straightforward enough, at least in rough outline. Nevertheless, it was rather different from anything that preceded it, and, somewhat more surprising, it disappeared almost without a trace as modern linguistics developed in the late nineteenth century. I want to say just a word about the relationship of the theory of deep and surface structure to earlier and later thinking about language.

There is a similarity, which I think can be highly misleading, between the theory of deep and surface structure and a much older tradition. The practitioners of philosophical grammar were very careful to stress this similarity in their detailed development of the theory and had no hesitation in expressing their debt to classical grammar as well as to such major figures of renaissance grammar as the Spanish scholar Sanctius. Sanctius, in particular, had developed a theory of ellipsis that had great influence on philosophical grammar. As I have already remarked, philosophical grammar is poorly understood today. But such antecedents as Sanctius have fallen into total oblivion. Furthermore, as in the case of all such work, there is a problem of determining not only what he said but also, more importantly, what he meant.

There is no doubt that in developing his concept of ellipsis as a fundamental property of language, Sanctius gave many linguistic examples that superficially are closely parallel to those that were used to develop the theory of deep and surface structure, both in classical philosophical grammar and in its far more explicit modern variants. It means, however, that the concept of ellipsis is intended by Sanctius merely as a device for the interpretation of texts. Thus, to determine the true meaning of an actual literary passage one must very often, according to Sanctius, regard it as an elliptical variant of a more elaborate paraphrase. But the Port-Royal theory and its later development, particularly at the hands of the encyclopedist Du Marsais, gave a rather different interpretation to ellipsis. The clear intent of philosophical grammar was to develop a psychological theory, not a technique of textual interpretation. The theory holds that the underlying deep structure, with its abstract organization of linguistic forms, is "present to the mind," as the signal, with its surface structure, is produced or perceived by the bodily organs. And the transformational operations relating deep and surface structure are actual mental operations, performed by the mind when a sentence is produced or understood. The distinction is fundamental. Under the latter interpretation, it follows that there must be, represented in the mind, a fixed system of generative principles that characterize and associate deep and surface structures in some definite way -- a grammar, in other words, that is used in some fashion as discourse is produced or interpreted. This grammar represents the underlying linguistic competence to which I referred earlier. The problem of determining the character of such grammars and the principles that govern them is a typical problem of science, perhaps very difficult, but in principle admitting of definite answers that are right or wrong as they do or do not correspond to the mental reality. But the theory of ellipsis as a technique of textual interpretation need not consist of a set of principles represented somehow in the mind as an aspect of normal human competence and intelligence. Rather, it can be in part ad hoc and can involve many cultural and personal factors relevant to the literary work under analysis.

The Port-Royal theory of deep and surface structure belongs to psychology as an attempt to elaborate Huarte's second type of wit, as an exploration of the properties of normal human intelligence. The concept ellipsis in Sanctius, if I understand it correctly, is one of many techniques, to be applied as conditions warrant and having no necessary mental representation as an aspect of a normal intelligence. Although the linguistic examples used are often similar, the context in which they are introduced and the framework in which they fit are fundamentally different in particular, they are separated by the Cartesian revolution. I propose this with some diffidence, because of the obscurity of the relevant and their intellectual backgrounds, but this interpretation seems to correct.

The relation of the Port-Royal theory to modern structural and descriptive linguistics is somewhat clearer. The latter restricts itself to the analysis of what I have called surface structure, to formal properties that are explicit in the signal and to phrases and units that can be determined from the signal by techniques of segmentation and classification. This restriction is a perfectly self-conscious one, and it was regarded -- I believe quite erroneously -- as a great advance. The great Swiss linguist Ferdinand de Saussure, who at the turn of the century laid the groundwork for modern structural linguistics, put forth the view that the only proper methods of linguistic analysis are segmentation and classification. Applying these methods, the linguist determines the patterns into which the units so analyzed fall, where these patterns are either syntagmatic -- that is, patterns of literal succession in the stream of speech -- or paradigmatic -- that is, relations among units that occupy the same position in the stream of speech. He held that when all such analysis is complete, the structure of the language is, of necessity, completely revealed, and the science of linguistics will have realized its task completely. Evidently, such taxonomic analysis leaves no place for deep structure in the sense of philosophical grammar. For example, the system of three propositions underlying the sentence "Invisible God created the visible world" cannot be derived from this sentence by segmentation and classification of segmented units, nor can the transformational operations relating the deep and surface structure, in this case, be expressed in terms of paradigmatic and syntagmatic structures. Modern structural linguistics has been faithful to these limitations, which were held to be necessary limitations.

In fact, Saussure in some respects even went beyond this in departing from the tradition of philosophical grammar. He occasionally expressed the view that processes of sentence formation do not belong to the system of language at all -- that the system of language is restricted to such linguistic units as sounds and words and perhaps a few fixed phrases and a small number of very general patterns; the mechanisms of sentence formation are otherwise free from any constraint imposed by linguistic structure as such. Thus, in his terms, sentence formation is not strictly a matter of *langue*, but is rather assigned to what he called *parole*, and thus placed outside the scope of linguistics proper; it is a process of free creation, unconstrained by linguistic rule except insofar as such rules govern the forms of words and the patterns of sounds. Syntax, in this view, is a rather trivial matter. And, in fact, there is very little work in syntax throughout the period of structural linguistics.

In taking this position, Saussure echoed an important critique of Humboldtian linguistic theory by the distinguished American linguist William Dwight Whitney, who evidently greatly influenced Saussure. According to Whitney, Humboldtian linguistic theory, which in many ways extended the Cartesian views that I have been discussing, was fundamentally in error. Rather, a language is simply "made up of a vast number of items, each of which has its own time, occasion, and effect." He maintained that "language in the concrete sense. . . is. . . the sum of words and phrases by which any man expresses his thought"; the task of the linguist, then, is to list these linguistic forms and to study their individual histories. In contrast to philosophical grammar, Whitney argued that there is nothing universal about the form of language and that one can learn nothing about the general properties of human intelligence from the study of the arbitrary agglomeration of forms that constitutes a human language. As he put it, "The infinite diversity of human speech ought alone to be a sufficient bar to the assertion that an understanding of the powers of the soul involves the explanation of speech." Similarly, Delbruck, in the standard work on Indo-European comparative syntax, denounced traditional grammar for having set up ideal sentence types underlying the observed signals, referring to Sanctius as the "major dogmatist in this domain."

With the expression of such sentiments as these, we enter the modern age of the study of language. The death-knell of philosophical grammar was sounded with the remarkable successes of comparative Indo-European studies, which surely rank among the outstanding achievements of nineteenth-century science. The impoverished and thoroughly inadequate conception of language expressed by Whitney and Saussure and numerous others proved to be entirely appropriate to the current stage of linguistic research. As a result, this conception was held to be vindicated, a not unnatural but thoroughly mistaken conviction. Modern structural-descriptive linguistics developed within the same intellectual framework and also made substantial progress, to which I will return directly. In contrast, philosophical grammar did not provide appropriate concepts for the new comparative grammar or for the study of exotic languages unknown to the investigator, and it was, in a sense, exhausted. It had reached the limits of what could be achieved within the framework of the ideas and techniques that were available. There was no clear understanding a century ago as to how one might proceed to construct generative grammars that "make infinite use of finite means" and that express the "organic form" of human language, "that marvellous invention" (in the words of the Port-Royal *Grammar*) "by which we construct from twenty-five or thirty sounds an infinity of expressions, which, having no resemblance in themselves to what takes place in our minds, still enable us to let others know the secret of what we conceive and of all the various mental activities that we carry out."

Thus, the study of language had arrived at a situation in which there was, on the one hand, a set of simple concepts that provided the basis for some startling successes and, on the other, some deep but rather vague ideas that did not seem to lead to any further productive research. The outcome was inevitable and not at all to be deplored. There developed a professionalization of the field, a shift of interest away from the classical problems of general interest to intellectuals like Arnauld and Humboldt, for example, toward a new domain largely defined by the techniques that the profession itself has forged in the solution of certain problems. Such a development is natural and quite proper, but not without its dangers. Without wishing to exalt the cult of gentlemanly amateurism, one must nevertheless recognize that the classical issues have a liveliness and significance that may be lacking in an area of investigation that is determined by the applicability of certain tools and methods, rather than by problems that are of intrinsic interest in themselves.

The moral is not to abandon useful tools; rather, it is, first, that one should maintain enough perspective to be able to detect the arrival of that inevitable day when the research that can be conducted with these tools is no longer important; and, second, that one should value ideas and insights that are to the point, though perhaps premature and vague and not productive of research at a particular stage of technique and understanding. With the benefits of hindsight, I think we can now see clearly that the disparagement and neglect of a rich tradition proved in the long run to be quite harmful to the study of language. Furthermore, this disparagement and neglect were surely unnecessary. Perhaps it would have been psychologically difficult, but there is no reason in principle why the successful exploitation of the structuralist approach in historical and descriptive study could not have been coupled with a clear recognition of its essential limitations and its ultimate inadequacy, in comparison with the tradition it temporarily, and quite justifiably, displaced. Here, I think, lies a lesson that may be valuable for the future study of language and mind.

To conclude, I think there have been two really productive traditions of research that have unquestionable relevance to anyone concerned with the study of language today. One is the tradition of philosophical grammar that flourished from the seventeenth century through romanticism; the second is the tradition that I have rather misleadingly been referring to as "structuralist," which has dominated research for the past century, at least until the early 1950's. I have dwelt on the achievements of the former because of their unfamiliarity as well as their contemporary relevance. Structural linguistics have enormously broadened the scope of information available to us and has extended immeasurably the reliability of such data. It has shown that there are structural relations in language that can be studied abstractly. It has raised the precision of discourse about language to entirely new levels. But I think that its major contribution may prove to be one for which, paradoxically, it has been very severely criticized. I refer to the careful and serious attempt to construct "discovery procedures," those techniques of segmentation and classification to which Saussure referred. This attempt was a failure -- I think that is now generally understood. It was a failure because such techniques are at best limited to the phenomena of surface structure and cannot, therefore, reveal the mechanisms that underlie the creative aspect of language use and the expression of semantic content. But what remains of fundamental importance is that this attempt was directed to the basic question in the study of language, which was for the first time formulated in a clear and intelligible way. The problem raised is that of specifying the mechanisms that operate on the data of sense and produce knowledge of language -- linguistic competence. It is obvious that such mechanisms exist. Children do learn a first language; the language that they learn is, in the traditional sense, an "instituted language," not an innately specified system. The answer that was proposed in structural linguistic methodology has been shown to be incorrect, but this is of small importance when compared with the fact that the problem itself has now received a clear formulation.

Whitehead once described the mentality of modern science as having been forged through "the union of passionate interest in the detailed facts with equal devotion to abstract generalization." It is roughly accurate to describe modern linguistics as passionately interested in detailed fact, and philosophical grammar as equally devoted to abstract generalization. It seems to me that the time has arrived to unite these two major currents and to develop a synthesis that will draw from their respective achievements. In the next two lectures, I will try to illustrate how the tradition of philosophical grammar can be reconstituted and turned to new and challenging problems and how one can, finally, return in a productive way to the basic questions and concerns that gave rise to this tradition.

LINGUISTIC CONTRIBUTIONS TO THE STUDY OF MIND--- Present

One difficulty in the psychological sciences lies in the familiarity of the phenomena with which they deal. A certain intellectual effort is required to see how such phenomena can pose serious problems or call for intricate explanatory theories. One is inclined to take them for granted as necessary or somehow "natural."

The effects of this familiarity of phenomena have often been discussed. Wolfgang Kohler, for example, has suggested that psychologists do not open up "entirely new territories" in the manner of the natural sciences, "simply because man was acquainted with practically all territories of mental life a long time before the founding of scientific psychology . . because at the very beginning of their work there were no entirely unknown mental facts left which they could have discovered."[1] The most elementary discoveries of classical physics have a certain shock value -- man has no intuition about elliptical orbits or the gravitational constant. But "mental facts" of even a much deeper sort cannot be "discovered" by the psychologist, because they are a matter of intuitive acquaintance and, once pointed out, are obvious.

There is also a more subtle effect. Phenomena can be so familiar that we really do not see them at all, a matter that has been much discussed by literary theorists and philosophers. For example, Viktor Shklovskij in the early 1920's developed the idea that the function of poetic art is that of "making strange" the object depicted. "People living at the seashore grow so accustomed to the murmur of the waves that they never hear it. By the same token, we scarcely ever hear the words which we utter. . . We look at each other, but we do not see each other any more. Our perception of the world has withered away; what has remained is mere recognition." Thus, the goal of the artist is to transfer what is depicted to the "sphere of new perception"; as an example, Shklovskij cites a story by Tolstoy in which social customs and institutions are "made strange" by the device of presenting them from the viewpoint of a narrator who happens to be a horse.[2]

---

[1] W. Kohler, *Dynamics* in *Psychology* (New York: Liveright, 1940).
[2] See V. Ehrlich, *Russian Formalism*, 2nd rev. ed. (New York: Humanities, 1965), pp.176-77.

The observation that "we look at each other, but we do not see each other any more" has perhaps itself achieved the status of "words which we utter but scarcely ever hear." But familiarity, in this case as well, should not obscure the importance of the insight.

Wittgenstein makes a similar observation, pointing out that "the aspects of things that are most important for us are hidden because of their simplicity and familiarity (one is unable to notice something -- because it is always before one's eyes)."[3] He sets himself to "supplying . . . remarks on the natural history of human beings: we are not contributing curiosities however, but observations which no one has doubted, but which have escaped remark only because they are always before our eyes."[4]

Less noticed is the fact that we also lose sight of the need for explanation when phenomena are too familiar and "obvious." We tend too easily to assume that explanations must be transparent and close to the surface. The greatest defect of classical philosophy of mind, both rationalist and empiricist, seems to me to be its unquestioned assumption that the properties and content of the mind are accessible to introspection; it is surprising to see how rarely this assumption has been challenged, insofar as the organization and function of the intellectual faculties are concerned, even with the Freudian revolution. Correspondingly, the farreaching studies of language that were carried out under the influence of Cartesian rationalism suffered from a failure to appreciate either the abstractness of those structures that are "present to the mind" when an utterance is produced or understood, or the length and complexity of the chain of operations that relate the mental structures expressing the semantic content of the utterance to the physical realization.

A similar defect mars the study of language and mind in the modern period. It seems to me that the essential weakness in the structuralist and behaviorist approaches to these topics is the faith in the shallowness of explanations, the belief that the mind must be simpler in its structure than any known physical organ and that the most primitive of assumptions must be adequate to explain whatever phenomena can be observed. Thus, it is taken for granted without argument or evidence (or is presented as true by definition) that a language is a "habit structure" or a network of associative connections, or that knowledge of language is merely a matter of "knowing how," a skill expressible as a system of dispositions to respond. Accordingly, knowledge of language must develop slowly through repetition and training, its apparent complexity resulting from the proliferation of very simple elements rather than from deeper principles of mental organization that may be as inaccessible to introspection as the

---

[3] Ludwig Wittgenstein, *Philosophical Investigations* (New York: Oxford University Press, 1953), Section 129.
[4] Ibid., Section 415.

mechanisms of digestion or coordinated movement. Although there is nothing inherently unreasonable in an attempt to account for knowledge and use of language in these terms, it also has no particular plausibility or a priori justification. There is no reason to react with uneasiness or disbelief if study of the knowledge of language and use of this knowledge should lead in an entirely different direction.

I think that in order to achieve progress in the study of language and human cognitive faculties in general it is necessary first to establish "psychic distance" from the "mental facts" to which Kohler referred, and then to explore the possibilities for developing explanatory theories, whatever they may suggest with regard to the complexity and abstractness of the underlying mechanisms. We must recognize that even the most familiar phenomena require explanation and that we have no privileged access to the underlying mechanisms, no more so than in physiology or physics. Only the most preliminary and tentative hypotheses can be offered concerning the nature of language, its use, and its acquisition. As native speakers, we have a vast amount of data available to us. For just this reason it is easy to fall into the trap of believing that there is nothing to be explained, that whatever organizing principles and underlying mechanisms may exist must be "given" as the data is given. Nothing could be further from the truth, and an attempt to characterize precisely the system of rules we have mastered that enables us to understand new sentences and produce a new sentence on an appropriate occasion will quickly dispel any dogmatism on this matter. The search for explanatory theories must begin with an attempt to determine these systems of rules and to reveal the principles that govern them.

The person who has acquired knowledge of a language has internalized a system of rules that relate sound and meaning in a particular way. The linguist constructing a grammar of a language is in effect proposing a hypothesis concerning this internalized system. The linguist's hypothesis, if presented with sufficient explicitness and precision, will have certain empirical consequences with regard to the form of utterances and their interpretations by the native speaker. Evidently, knowledge of language -- the internalized system of rules -- is only one of the many factors that determine how an utterance will be used or understood in a particular situation. The linguist who is trying to determine what constitutes knowledge of a language -- to construct a correct grammar -- is studying one fundamental factor that is involved in performance, but not the only one. This idealization must be kept in mind when one is considering the problem of confirmation of grammars on the basis of empirical evidence. There is no reason why one should not also study the interaction of several factors involved in complex mental acts and underlying actual performance, but such a study is not likely to proceed very far unless the separate factors are themselves fairly well understood.

In a good sense, the grammar proposed by the linguist is an explanatory theory; it suggests an explanation for the fact that (under the idealization mentioned) a speaker of the language in question will perceive, interpret, form, or use an utterance in certain ways and not in other ways. One can also search for explanatory theories of a deeper sort. The native speaker has acquired a grammar on the basis of very restricted and degenerate evidence; the grammar has empirical consequences that extend far beyond the evidence. At one level, the phenomena with which the grammar deals are explained by the rules of the grammar itself and the interaction of these rules. At a deeper level, these same phenomena are explained by the principles that determine the selection of the grammar on the basis of the restricted and degenerate evidence available to the person who has acquired knowledge of the language, who has constructed for himself this particular grammar. The principles that determine the form of grammar and that select a grammar of the appropriate form on the basis of certain data constitute a subject that might, following a traditional usage, be termed "universal grammar. The study of universal grammar, so understood, is a study of the nature of human intellectual capacities. It tries to formulate the necessary and sufficient conditions that a system must meet to qualify as a potential human language, conditions that are not accidentally true of the existing human languages, but that are rather rooted in the human "language capacity," and thus constitute the innate organization that determines what counts as linguistic experience and what knowledge of language arises on the basis of this experience. Universal grammar, then, constitutes an explanatory theory of a much deeper sort than particular grammar, although the particular grammar of a language can also be regarded as an explanatory theory.[5]

In practice, the linguist is always involved in the study of both universal and particular grammar. When he constructs a descriptive, particular grammar in one way rather than another on the basis of what evidence he has available, he is guided, consciously or not, by certain assumptions as to the form of grammar, and these assumptions belong to the theory of universal grammar. Conversely, his formulation of principles of universal grammar must be justified by the study of their consequences when applied in particular grammars. Thus, at several levels the linguist is involved in the construction of explanatory theories, and at each level there is a clear psychological interpretation for his theoretical and descriptive work. At the level of particular grammar, he is attempting to characterize knowledge of a language, a certain cognitive system that has been

---

[5] To bring out this difference in depth of explanation, I have suggested in my *Current Issues in Linguistic Theory* (New York: Humanities, 1964) that the term "level of descriptive adequacy" might be used for the study of the relation between grammars and data and the term "level of explanatory adequacy" for the relation between a theory of universal grammar and these data.

developed -- unconsciously, of course -- by the normal speaker-hearer. At the level of universal grammar, he is trying to establish certain general properties of human intelligence. Linguistics, so characterized, is simply the subfield of psychology that deals with these aspects of mind.

LINGUISTIC CONTRIBUTIONS TO THE STUDY OF MIND -- Future

In discussing the past, I referred to two major traditions that have enriched the study of language in their separate and very different ways; and in my last lecture, I tried to give some indication of the topics that seem on the immediate horizon today, as a kind of synthesis of philosophical grammar and structural linguistics begins to take shape. Each of the major traditions of study and speculation that I have been using as a point of reference was associated with a certain characteristic approach to the problems of mind; we might say, without distortion, that each evolved as a specific branch of the psychology of its time, to which it made a distinctive contribution.

It may seem a bit paradoxical to speak of structural linguistics in this way, given its militant anti-psychologism. But the paradox is lessened when we take note of the fact that this militant anti-psychologism is no less true of much of contemporary psychology itself, particularly of those branches that until a few years ago monopolized the study of use and acquisition of language. We live, after all, in the age of "behavioral science," not of "the science of mind." I do not want to read too much into a terminological innovation, but I think that there is some significance in the ease and willingness with which modern thinking about man and society accepts the designation "behavioral science." No sane person has ever doubted that behavior provides much of the evidence for this study -- all of the evidence, if we interpret "behavior" in a sufficiently loose sense. But the term "behavioral science" suggests a not-so-subtle shift of emphasis toward the evidence itself and away from the deeper underlying principles and abstract mental structures that might be illuminated by the evidence of behavior. It is as if natural science were to be designated "the science of meter readings." What, in fact, would we expect of natural science in a culture that was satisfied to accept this designation for its activities?

Behavioral science has been much preoccupied with data and organization of data; and it has even seen itself as a kind of technology of control of behavior. Anti-mentalism in linguistics and in philosophy of language conforms to this shift of orientation. As I mentioned in my first lecture, I think that one major indirect contribution of modern structural linguistics results from its success in making explicit the assumptions of an anti-mentalistic, thoroughly operational and behaviorist approach to the phenomena of language. By extending this approach to its natural limits, it laid the groundwork for a fairly conclusive demonstration of the inadequacy of any such approach to the problems of mind.

More generally, I think that the long-range significance of the study of language lies in the fact that in this study it is possible to give a relatively sharp and clear formulation of some of the central questions of psychology and to bring a mass of evidence to bear on them. What is more, the study of language is, for the moment, unique in the combination it affords of richness of data and susceptibility to sharp formulation of basic issues.

It would, of course, be silly to try to predict the future of research, and it will be understood that I do not intend the subtitle of this lecture to be taken very seriously. Nevertheless, it is fair to suppose that the major contribution of the study of language will lie in the understanding it can provide as to the character of mental processes and the structures they form and manipulate. Therefore, instead of speculating on the likely course of research into the problems that are coming into focus today,[1] I will concentrate here on some of the issues that arise when we try to develop the study of linguistic structure as a chapter of human psychology.

It is quite natural to expect that a concern for language will remain central to the study of human nature, as it has been in the past. Anyone concerned with the study of human nature and human capacities must somehow come to grips with the fact that all normal humans acquire language, whereas acquisition of even it's barest rudiments is quite beyond the capacities of an otherwise intelligent ape -- a fact that was emphasized, quite correctly, in Cartesian philosophy.[2] It is widely thought that the extensive modern studies of animal

---

[1] A number of such problems might be enumerated--for example, the problem of how the intrinsic content of phonetic features determines the functioning of phonological rules, the role of universal formal conditions in restricting the choice of grammars and the empirical interpretation of such grammars, the relations of syntactic and semantic structure, the nature of universal semantics, performance models that incorporate generative grammars, and so on.

[2] Modern attempts to train apes in behavior 'that the investigators regard as Language-like confirm this incapacity, though it may be that the failures are to be attributed to the technique of operant conditioning and therefore show little about the animal's actual abilities. See, for example, the report by C. B. Ferster, "Arithmetic Behavior in Chimpanzees," in Scientific American, May 1964, pp. 9-106. Ferster attempted to teach chimpanzees to match the binary numbers 001,...,111 to sets of one to seven objects. He reports that hundreds of thousands of trials were required for 95 per cent accuracy to be achieved, even in this trivial task. Of course, even at this stage the apes had not learned the principle of binary arithmetic; they would not, for example, be able to match a four-digit binary number correctly, and, presumably, they would have done just as badly in the experiment had it involved an arbitrary association of the binary numbers to sets rather than the association determined 'by the principle (of the binary notation. Ferster overlooks this crucial point and therefore includes, mistakenly, that he has taught the rudiments of symbolic behavior. The confusion is compounded by his definition of language as "a set of symbolic stimuli that control behavior" and by his strange belief that the "effectiveness" of language arises from the fact that utterances "control almost identical performances in speaker and listener."

communication challenge this classical view; and it is almost universally taken for granted that there exists a problem of explaining the "evolution" of human language from systems of animal communication. However, a careful look at recent studies of animal communication seems to me to provide little support for these assumptions. Rather, these studies simply bring out even more clearly the extent to which human language appears to be a unique phenomenon, without significant analogue in the animal world. If this is so, it is quite senseless to raise the problem of explaining the evolution of human language from more primitive systems of communication that appear at lower levels of intellectual capacity. The issue is important, and I would like to dwell on it for a moment.

The assumption that human language evolved from more primitive systems is developed in an interesting way by Karl Popper in his recently published Arthur Compton Lecture, "Clouds and Clocks." He tries to show how problems of freedom of will and Cartesian dualism can be solved by the analysis of this "evolution." I am not concerned now with the philosophical conclusions that he draws from this analysis, but with the basic assumption that there is an evolutionary development of language from simpler systems of the sort that one discovers in other organisms. Popper argues that the evolution of language passed through several stages, in particular a "lower stage" in which vocal gestures are used for expression of emotional state, for example, and a "higher stage" in which articulated sound is used for expression (of thought -- in Popper's terms, for description and critical argument. His discussion of stages of evolution of language suggests a kind of continuity, but in fact he establishes no relation between the lower and higher stages and does not suggest a mechanism whereby transition can take place from one stage to the next. In short, he gives no argument to show that the stages belong to a single evolutionary process. In fact, it is difficult to see what links these stages at all (except for the metaphorical use of the term "language"). There is no reason to suppose that the "gaps" are bridgeable. There is no more of a basis for assuming an evolutionary development of "higher" from "lower" stages, in this case, than there is for assuming an evolutionary development from breathing to walking; the stages have no significant analogy, it appears, and seem to involve entirely different processes and principles.

A more explicit discussion of the relation between human language and animal communication systems appears in a recent discussion by the comparative ethologist W. H. Thorpe.[3] He points out that mammals other than man appear to lack the human ability to imitate sounds, and that one might therefore have expected birds (many of which have this ability to a remarkable extent) to be "the group which ought to have been able to evolve language in the true sense, and not the mammals." Thorpe does not suggest that human language "evolved" in any strict sense from simpler systems, but he does argue

---

[3] W. H. Thorpe, "Animal Vocalization and Communication," in F. L. Darley, ed., Brain Mechanisms Underlying Speech and Language (New York: Grune and Stratton, 1967), pp.2-10 and the discussions on pp.19 and 84-85.

that the characteristic properties of human language can be found in animal communication systems, although "we cannot at the moment say definitely that they are all present in one particular animal." The characteristics shared by human and animal language are the properties of being "purposive," syntactic," and propositional." Language is purposive "in that there is nearly always in human speech a definite intention of getting something over to somebody else, altering his behavior, his thoughts, or his general attitude toward a situation." Human language is "syntactic" in that an utterance is a performance with an internal organization, with structure and coherence. It is "propositional" in that it transmits information. In this sense, then, both human language and animal communication are purposive, syntactic, and propositional.

All this may be true, but it establishes very little, since when we move to the level of abstraction at which human language and animal communication fall together, almost all other behavior is included as well. Consider walking: Clearly, walking is purposive behavior, in the most general sense of "purposive." Walking is also "syntactic" in the sense just defined, as, in fact, Karl Lashley pointed out a long time ago in his important discussion of serial order in behavior, to which I referred in the first lecture.

[4] Furthermore, it can certainly be informative; for example, I can signal my interest in reaching a certain goal by the speed or intensity with which I walk.

It is, incidentally, precisely in this manner that the examples of animal communication that Thorpe presents are "propositional." He cites as an example the song of the European robin, in which the rate of alternation of high and low pitch signals the intention of the bird to defend its territory; the higher the rate of alternation, the greater the intention to defend the territory. The example is interesting, but it seems to me to show very clearly the hopelessness of the attempt to relate human language to animal communication. Every animal communication system that is known (if we disregard some science fiction about dolphins) uses one of two basic principles: Either it consists of a fixed, finite number of signals, each associated with a specific range of behavior or emotional state, as is illustrated in the extensive primate studies that have been carried out by Japanese scientists for the past several years; or it makes use of a fixed, finite number of linguistic dimensions, each of which is associated with a particular nonlinguistic dimension in such a way that selection of a point along the linguistic dimension determines and signals a certain point along the associated nonlinguistic dimension. The latter is the principle realized in Thorpe's bird-song example. Rate of alternation of high and low pitch is a linguistic dimension correlated with the non-linguistic dimension of intention to defend a territory. The bird signals its intention to defend a territory by selecting a correlated point along the linguistic dimension of pitch alternation -- I use the word "select" loosely, of course. The linguistic dimension is abstract, but the prin-

---

[4] K. S. Lashley, "The Problem of Serial Order in Behavior," in L. A. Jeffress, ed., *Cerebral Mechanisms in Behavior* (New York: Wiley, 1951), pp.112-36.

ciple is clear. A communication system of the second type has an indefinitely large range of potential signals, as does human language. The mechanism and principle, however, are entirely different from those employed by human language to express indefinitely many new thoughts, intentions, feelings, and so on. It is not correct to speak of a "deficiency" of the animal system, in terms of range of potential signals; rather the opposite, since the animal system admits in principle of continuous variation along the linguistic dimension (insofar as it makes sense to speak of "continuity" in such a case), whereas human language is discrete. Hence, the issue is not one of "more" or "less," but rather of an entirely different principle of organization. When I make some arbitrary statement in a human language -- say, that "the rise of supranational corporations poses new dangers for human freedom" -- I am not selecting a point along some linguistic dimension that signals a corresponding point along an associated nonlinguistic dimension, nor am I selecting a signal from a finite behavioral repertoire, innate or learned.

Furthermore, it is wrong to think of human use of language as characteristically informative, in fact or in intention. Human language can be used to inform or mislead, to clarify one's own thoughts or to display one's cleverness, or simply for play. If I speak with no concern for modifying your behavior or thoughts, I am not using language any less than if I say exactly the same things *with* such intention. If we hope to understand human language and the psychological capacities on which it rests, we must first ask what it is, not how or for what purposes it is used. When we ask what human language is, we find no striking similarity to animal communication systems. There is nothing useful to be said about behavior or thought at the level of abstraction at which animal and human communication fall together. The examples of animal communication that have been examined to date do share many of the properties of human gestural systems, and it might be reasonable to explore the possibility of direct connection in this case. But human language, it appears, is based on entirely different principles. This, I think, is an important point, often overlooked by those who approach human language as a natural, biological phenomenon; in particular, it seems rather pointless, for these reasons, to speculate about the evolution of human language from simpler systems -- perhaps as absurd as it would be to speculate about the "evolution" of atoms from clouds of elementary particles.

As far as we know, possession of human language is associated with a specific type of mental organization, not simply a higher degree of intelligence. There seems to be no substance to the view that human language is simply a more complex instance of something to be found elsewhere in the animal world. This poses a problem for the biologist, since, if true, it is an example of true "emergence" -- the appearance of a qualitatively different phenomenon at a specific stage of complexity of organization. Recognition of this fact, though formulated in entirely different terms, is what motivated much of the classical study of language by those whose primary concern was the nature of mind. And it seems to me that today there is no better or more promising way to explore the essential and distinctive properties of human intelligence than through the detailed investigation of the structure of this unique human possession. A reasonable guess, then, is that if empirically adequate generative grammars can be constructed and the universal principles that govern their structure and organization determined, then this will be an important contribution to human psychology, in ways to which I will turn directly, in detail.

In the course of these lectures I have mentioned some of the classical ideas regarding language structure and contemporary efforts to deepen and extend them. It seems clear that we must regard linguistic competence -- knowledge of a language -- as an abstract system underlying behavior, a system constituted by rules that interact to determine the form and intrinsic meaning of a potentially infinite number of sentences. Such a system -- a generative grammar -- provides an explication of the Humboldtian idea of "form of language," which in an obscure but suggestive remark in his great posthumous work, Uber die Verschiedenheit des Menschilichen Sprachbaues, Humboldt defines as "that constant and unvarying system of processes underlying the mental act of raising articulated structurally organized signals to an expression of thought." Such a grammar defines a language in the Humboldtian sense, namely as "a recursively generated system, where the laws of generation are fixed and invariant, but the scope and the specific manner in which they are applied remain entirely unspecified."

In each such grammar there are particular, idiosyncratic elements, selection of which determines one specific human language; and there are general universal elements, conditions on the form and organization of any human language, that form the subject matter for the study of universal grammar." Among the principles of universal grammar are those I discussed in the preceding lecture -- for example, the principles that distinguish deep and surface structure and that constrain the class of transformational operations that relate them. Notice, incidentally, that the existence of definite principles of universal grammar makes possible the rise of the new field of mathematical linguistics, a field that submits to abstract study the class of generative systems meeting the conditions set forth in universal grammar. This inquiry aims to elaborate the formal properties of any possible human language. The field is in its infancy; it is only in the last decade that the possibility of such an enterprise has been envisioned. It has some promising initial results, and it suggests one possible direction for future research that might prove to be of great importance. Thus, mathematical linguistics seems for the moment to be in a uniquely favorable position, among mathematical approaches in the social and psychological sciences, to develop not simply as a theory of data, but as the study of highly abstract principles and structures that determine the character of human mental processes. In this case, the mental processes in question are those involved in the organization of one specific domain of human knowledge, namely knowledge of language.

The theory of generative grammar, both particular and universal, points to a conceptual lacuna in psychological theory that I believe is worth mentioning. Psychology conceived as "behavioral science" has been concerned with behavior and acquisition or control of behavior. It has no concept corresponding to "competence," in the sense in which competence is characterized by a generative grammar. The theory of learning has limited itself to a narrow and surely inadequate concept of what is learned -- namely a system of stimulus-response connections, a network of associations, a repertoire of behavioral items, a habit hierarchy, or a system of dispositions to respond in a particular way under specifiable stimulus conditions.[5] Insofar as behavioral psychology has been applied to education or therapy, it has correspondingly limited itself to this concept of "what is learned." But a generative grammar cannot be characterized in these terms. What is necessary, in addition to the concept of behavior and learning, is a concept of what is learned -- a notion of competence -- that lies beyond the conceptual limits of behaviorist psychological theory. Like much of modern linguistics and modern philosophy of language, behaviorist psychology has quite consciously accepted methodological restrictions that do not permit the study of systems of the necessary complexity and abstractness.[6] One important future contribution of the study of language to general psychology may be to focus attention on this conceptual gap and to demonstrate how it may be filled by the elaboration of a system of underlying competence in one domain of human intelligence.

---

[5] This limitation is revealed, for example, in such statements as this from W. M. Wiest, in "Recent Criticisms of Behaviorism and Learning," in Psychological Bulletin, Vol.67, No.3, 1967, pp.214-25: "An empirical demonstration ... that a child has learned the rules of grammar would be his exhibiting the verbal performance called 'uttering the rules of grammar.' That this performance is not usually acquired without special training is attested to by many grammar school teachers. One may even speak quite grammatically without having literally learned the rules of grammar." Wiest's inability to conceive of another sense in which the child may be said to have learned the rules of grammar testifies to the conceptual gap we are discussing. Since he refuses to consider the question of what is learned, and to clarify this notion before asking how it is learned, he can only conceive of "grammar" as the "behavioral regularities in the understanding and production of speech" -- a characterization that is perfectly empty, as it stands, there being no "behavioral regularities" associated with (let alone "in") the understanding and production of speech. One cannot quarrel with the desire of some investigators to study "the acquisition and maintenance of actual occurrences of verbal behavior" (ibid.). It remains to be demonstrated that this study has something to do with the study of language. As of now, I see no indication that this claim can be substantiated.

[6] See my paper, "Some Empirical Assumptions in Modern Philosophy of Language," in S. Morgenbesser, P. Suppes, and M. White, eds., Essays in Honor of Ernest Nagel (New York: St. Martin's, 1969), for a discussion of the work of Quine and Wittgenstein from this point of view.

There is an obvious sense in which any aspect of psychology is based ultimately on the observation of behavior. But it is not at all obvious that the study of learning should proceed directly to the investigation of factors that control behavior or of conditions under which a "behavioral repertoire" is established. It is first necessary to determine the significant characteristics of this behavioral repertoire, the principles on which it is organized. A meaningful study of learning can proceed only after this preliminary task has been carried out and has led to a reasonably well-confirmed theory of underlying competence -- in the case of language, to the formulation of the generative grammar that underlies the observed use of language. Such a study will concern itself with the relation between the data available to the organism and the competence that it acquires; only to the extent that the abstraction to competence has been successful -- in the case of language, to the extent that the postulated grammar is "descriptively adequate" in the sense described in Lecture 2 -- can the investigation of learning hope to achieve meaningful results. If, in some domain, the organization of the behavioral repertoire is quite trivial and elementary, then there will be little harm in avoiding the intermediate stage of theory construction, in which we attempt to characterize accurately the competence that is acquired. But one cannot count on this being the case, and in the study of language it surely is not the case. With a richer and more adequate characterization of "what is learned" -- of the underlying competence that constitutes the "final state" of the organism being studied -- it may be possible to approach the task of constructing a theory of learning that will be much less restricted in scope than modern behavioral psychology has proved to be. Surely it is pointless to accept methodological strictures that preclude such an approach to problems of learning.

Are there other areas of human competence where one might hope to develop a fruitful theory, analogous to generative grammar? Although this is a very important question, there is very little that can be said about it today. One might, for example, consider the problem of how a person comes to acquire a certain concept of three-dimensional space, or an implicit "theory of human action," in similar terms. Such a study would begin with the attempt to characterize the implicit theory that underlies actual performance and would then turn to the question of how this theory develops under the given conditions of time and access to data -- that is, in what way the resulting system of beliefs is determined by the interplay of available data, "heuristic procedures," and the innate schematism that restricts and conditions the form of the acquired system. At the moment, this is nothing more than a sketch of a program of research.

There have been some attempts to study the structure of other, language-like systems -- the study of kinship systems and folk taxonomies comes to mind, for example. But so far, at least, nothing has been discovered that is even roughly comparable to language in these domains. No one, to my knowledge, has devoted more thought to this problem than Levi-Strauss. For example, his recent book on the categories of primitive mentality[7] is a serious and thoughtful attempt to come to grips with this problem. Nevertheless, I do not see what conclusions can be reached from a study of his materials beyond the fact that the savage mind attempts to impose some organization on the physical world -- that humans classify, if they perform any mental acts at all. Specifically, Levi-Strauss's well-known critique of totemism seems to reduce to little more than this conclusion.

Levi-Strauss models his investigations quite consciously on structural linguistics, particularly on the work of Troubetzkoy and Jakobson. He repeatedly and quite correctly emphasizes that one cannot simply apply procedures analogous to those of phonemic analysis to subsystems of society and culture. Rather, he is concerned with structures "where they may be found. . . in the kinship system, political ideology, mythology, ritual, art," and so on,[8] and he wishes to examine the formal properties of these structures in their own terms. But several reservations are necessary when structural linguistics is used as a model in this way. For one thing, the structure of a phonological system is of very little interest as a formal object; there is nothing of significance to be said, from a formal point of view, about a set of forty-odd elements cross-classified in terms of eight or ten features. The significance of structuralist phonology, as developed by Troubetzkoy, Jakobson, and others, lies not in the formal properties of phonemic systems but in the fact that a fairly small number of features that can be specified in absolute, language-independent terms appear to provide the basis for the organization of all phonological systems. The achievement of structuralist phonology was to show that the phonological rules of a great variety of languages apply to classes of elements that can be simply characterized in terms of these features; that historical change affects such classes in a uniform way; and that the organization of features plays a basic role in the use and acquisition of language. This was a discovery of the greatest importance, and it provides the groundwork for much of contemporary linguistics. But if we abstract away from the specific universal set of features and the rule systems in which they function, little of any significance remains.

Furthermore, to a greater and greater extent, current work in phonology is demonstrating that the real richness of phonological systems lies not in the structural patterns of phonemes but rather in the intricate systems of rules by which these patterns are formed, modified, and elaborated.[9] The structural patterns that arise at various stages of derivation are a kind of epiphenomenon. The system of phonological rules makes use of the universal features in a fundamental way,[10] but it is the properties of the systems of rules, it seems to me,

---

[7] C. Levi-Strauss, *The Savage Mind* (Chicago University of Chicago Press, 1967).
[8] C. Levi-Strauss, *Structural Anthropology* (New York: Basic Books, 1963); p.85.
[9] See discussion in the preceding lecture and the references cited there.
[10] The study of universal features is itself in considerable flux. See N. Chomsky and M. Halle, *The Sound Pattern of English* (New York: Harper & Row, 1968), Chapter 7, for recent discussion.

that really shed light on the specific nature of the organization of language. For example, there appear to be very general conditions, such as the principle of cyclic ordering (discussed in the preceding lecture) and others that are still more abstract, that govern the application of these rules, and there are many interesting and unsolved questions as to how the choice of rules is determined by intrinsic, universal relations among features. Furthermore, the idea of a mathematical investigation of language structures, to which Levi-Strauss occasionally alludes, becomes meaningful only when one considers systems of rules with infinite generative capacity. There is nothing to be said about the abstract structure of the various patterns that appear at various stages of derivation. If this is correct, then one cannot expect structuralist phonology, in itself, to provide a useful model for investigation of other cultural and social systems.

In general, the problem of extending concepts of linguistic structure to other cognitive systems seems to me, for the moment, in not too promising a state, although it is no doubt too early for pessimism.

Before turning to the general implications of the study of linguistic competence and, more specifically, to the conclusions of universal grammar, it is well to make sure of the status of these conclusions in the light of current knowledge of the possible diversity of language. In my first lecture, I quoted the remarks of William Dwight Whitney about what he referred to as "the infinite diversity of human speech," the boundless variety that, he maintained, undermines the claims of philosophical grammar to psychological relevance.

Philosophical grammarians had typically maintained that languages vary little in their deep structures, though there may be wide variability in surface manifestations. Thus there is, in this view, an underlying structure of grammatical relations and categories, and certain aspects of human thought and mentality are essentially invariant across languages, although languages may differ as to whether they express the grammatical relations formally by inflection or word order, for example. Furthermore, an investigation of their work indicates that the underlying recursive principles that generate deep structure were assumed to be restricted in certain ways -- for example, by the condition that new structures are formed only by the insertion of new "propositional content," new structures that themselves correspond to actual simple sentences, in fixed positions in already formed structures. Similarly, the grammatical transformations that form surface structures through reordering, ellipsis, and other formal operations must themselves meet certain fixed general conditions, such as those discussed in the preceding lecture. In short, the theories of philosophical grammar, and the more recent elaborations of these theories, make the assumption that languages will differ very little, despite considerable diversity in superficial realization, when we discover their deeper structures and unearth their fundamental mechanisms and principles.

It is interesting to observe that this assumption persisted even through the period of German romanticism, which was, of course, much preoccupied with the diversity of cultures and with the many rich possibilities For human intellectual development. Thus, Wilhelm von Humboldt, who is now best remembered for his ideas concerning the variety of languages and the association of diverse language structures with divergent "world-views," nevertheless held firmly that underlying any human language we will find a system that is universal, that simply expresses man's unique intellectual attributes. For this reason, it was possible for him to maintain the rationalist view that language is not really learned -- certainly not taught -- but rather develops "from within," in an essentially predetermined way, when the appropriate environmental conditions exist. One cannot really teach a first language, he argued, but can only "provide the thread along which it will develop of its own accord," by processes more like maturation than learning. This Platonistic element in Humboldt's thought is a pervasive one; for Humboldt, it was as natural to propose an essentially Platonistic theory of "learning" as it was for Rousseau to found his critique of repressive social institutions on a conception of human freedom that derives from strictly Cartesian assumptions regarding the limitations of mechanical explanation. And in general it seems appropriate to construe both the psychology and the linguistics of the romantic period as in large part a natural outgrowth of rationalist conceptions.[11]

The issue raised by Whitney against Humboldt and philosophical grammar in general is of great significance with respect to the implications of linguistics for general human psychology. Evidently, these implications can be truly far-reaching only if the rationalist view is essentially correct, in which case the structure of language can truly serve as a "mirror of mind," in both its particular and its universal aspects. It is widely believed that modern anthropology has established the falsity of the assumptions of the rationalist universal grammarians by demonstrating through empirical study that languages may, in fact, exhibit the widest diversity. Whitney's claims regarding the diversity of languages are reiterated throughout the modern period; Martin Joos, for example, is simply expressing the conventional wisdom when he takes the basic conclusion of modern anthropological linguistics to be that "languages can differ without limit as to either extent or direction."[12]

---

[11] For some discussion of these matters, see my *Cartesian Linguistics* (New York: Harper & Row, 1966).

[12] M. Joos, ed., Readings in Linguistics, 4th ed. (Chicago: University of Chicago Press, 1966), p.228. This is put forth as the "Boas Tradition." American linguistics, Joos maintains, "got its decisive direction when it was decided that an indigenous language could be described without any preexistent scheme of what a language must be...." (p. 1). Of course this could not literally be true -- the procedures of analysis themselves express a hypothesis concerning the possible diversity of language. But there is, nevertheless, much justice in Joos's characterization.

The belief that anthropological linguistics has demolished the assumptions of universal grammar seems to me to be quite false in two important respects. First, it misinterprets the views of classical rationalist grammar, which held that languages are similar only at the deeper level, the level at which grammatical relations are expressed and at which the processes that provide for the creative aspect of language use are to be found. Second, this belief seriously misinterprets the findings of anthropological linguistics, which has, in fact, restricted itself almost completely to fairly superficial aspects of language structure.

To say this is not to criticize anthropological linguistics, a field that is faced with compelling problems of its own -- in particular, the problem of obtaining at least some record of the rapidly vanishing languages of the primitive world. Nevertheless, it is important to bear in mind this fundamental limitation on its achievements in considering the light it can shed on the theses of universal grammar. Anthropological studies (like structural linguistic studies in general) do not attempt to reveal the underlying core of generative processes in language -- that is, the processes that determine the deeper levels of structure and that constitute the systematic means for creating ever novel sentence types. Therefore, they obviously cannot have any real bearing on the classical assumption that these underlying generative processes vary only slightly from language to language. In fact, what evidence is now available suggests that if universal grammar has serious defects, as indeed it does from a modern point of view, then these defects lie in the failure to recognize the abstract nature of linguistic structure and to impose sufficiently strong and restrictive conditions on the form of any human language. And a characteristic feature of current work in linguistics is its concern for linguistic universals of a sort that can only be detected through a detailed investigation of particular languages, universals governing properties of language that are simply not accessible to investigation within the restricted framework that has been adopted, often for very good reasons, within anthropological linguistics.

I think that if we contemplate the classical problem of psychology, that of accounting for human knowledge; we cannot avoid being struck by the enormous disparity between knowledge and experience -- in the case of language, between the generative grammar that expresses the linguistic competence of the native speaker and the meager and degenerate data on the basis of which he has constructed this grammar for himself. In principle the theory of learning should deal with this problem; but in fact it bypasses the problem, because of the conceptual gap that I mentioned earlier. The problem cannot even be formulated in any sensible way until we develop the concept of competence, alongside the concepts of learning and behavior, and apply this concept in some domain. The fact is that this concept has so far been extensively developed and applied only in the study of human language. It is only in this domain that we have at least the first steps toward an account of competence, namely the fragmentary generative grammars that have been constructed for particular languages. As the study of language progresses, we can expect with some confidence that these grammars will be extended in scope and depth, although it will hardly come as a surprise if the first proposals are found to be mistaken in fundamental ways.

Insofar as we have a tentative first approximation to a generative grammar for some language, we can for the first time formulate in a useful way the problem of origin of knowledge. In other words, we can ask the question, What initial structure must be attributed to the mind that enables it to construct such a grammar from the data of sense? Some of the empirical conditions that must be met by any such assumption about innate structure are moderately clear. Thus, it appears to be a species-specific capacity that is essentially independent of intelligence, and we can make a fairly good estimate of the amount of data that is necessary for the task to be successfully accomplished. We know that the grammars that are in fact constructed vary only slightly among speakers of the same language, despite wide variations not only in intelligence but also in the conditions under which language is acquired. As participants in a certain culture, we are naturally aware of the great differences in ability to use language, in knowledge of vocabulary, and so on that result from differences in native ability and from differences in conditions of acquisition; we naturally pay much less attention to the similarities and to common knowledge, which we take for granted. But if we manage to establish the requisite psychic distance, if we actually compare the generative grammars that must be postulated for different speakers of the same language, we find that the similarities that we take for granted are quite marked and that the divergences are few and marginal. What is more, it seems that dialects that are superficially quite remote, even barely intelligible on first contact, share a vast central core of common rules and processes and differ very slightly in underlying structures, which seem to remain invariant through long historical eras. Furthermore, we discover a substantial system of principles that do not vary among languages that are, as far as we know, entirely unrelated.

  The central problems in this domain are empirical ones that are, in principle at least, quite straightforward, difficult as they may be to solve in a satisfactory way. We must postulate an innate structure that is rich enough to account for the disparity between experience and knowledge, one that can account for the construction of the empirically justified generative grammars within the given limitations of time and access to data. At the same time, this postulated innate mental structure must not be so rich and restrictive as to exclude certain known languages. There is, in other words, an upper bound and a lower bound on the degree and exact character of the complexity that can be postulated as innate mental structure. The factual situation is obscure enough to leave room for much difference of opinion over the true nature of this innate mental structure that makes acquisition of language possible. However, there seems to me to be no doubt that this is an empirical issue, one that can be resolved by proceeding along the lines that I have just roughly outlined.

My own estimate of the situation is that the real problem for tomorrow is that of discovering an assumption regarding innate structure that is sufficiently rich, not that of finding one that is simple or elementary enough to be "plausible." There is, as far as I can see, no reasonable notion of "plausibility," no a priori insight into what innate structures are permissible, that can guide the search for a "sufficiently elementary assumption." It would be mere dogmatism to maintain without argument or evidence that the mind is simpler in its innate structure than other biological systems, just as it would be mere dogmatism to insist that the mind's organization must necessarily follow certain set principles, determined in advance of investigation and maintained in defiance of any empirical findings. I think that the study of problems of mind has been very definitely hampered by a kind of apriorism with which these problems are generally approached. In particular, the empiricist assumptions that have dominated the study of acquisition of knowledge for many years seem to me to have been adopted quite without warrant and to have no special status among the many possibilities that one might imagine as to how the mind functions.

FORM AND MEANING
IN NATURAL LANGUAGES

When we study human language, we are approaching what some might call the "human essence, the distinctive qualities of mind that are, so far as we know, unique to man and that are inseparable from any critical phase of human existence, personal or social Hence the fascination of this study, and, no less, its frustration. The frustration arises from the fact that despite much progress, we remain as incapable as ever before of coming to grips with the core problem of human language, which I take to be this: Having mastered a language, one is able to understand an indefinite number of expressions that are new to one's experience, that bear no simple physical resemblance and are in no simple way analogous to the expressions that constitute one's linguistic experience; and one is able, with greater or less facility, to produce such expressions on an appropriate occasion, despite their novelty and independently of detectable stimulus configurations, and to be understood by others who share this still mysterious ability. The normal use of language is, in this sense, a creative activity. This creative aspect of normal language use is one fundamental factor that distinguishes human language from any known system of animal communication.

It is important to bear in mind that the creation of linguistic expressions that are novel but appropriate is the normal mode of language use. If some individual were to restrict himself largely to a definite set of linguistic patterns, to a set of habitual responses to stimulus configurations, or to "analogies" in the sense of modern linguistics, we would regard him as mentally defective, as being less human than animal. He would immediately be set apart from normal humans by his inability to understand normal discourse, or to take part in it in the normal way -- the normal way being innovative free from control by external stimuli, and appropriate to new and ever changing situations.

It is not a novel insight that human speech is distinguished by these qualities, though it is an insight that must be recaptured time and time again. With each advance in our understanding of the mechanisms of language, thought, and behavior, comes a tendency to believe that we have found the key to understanding man's apparently unique qualities of mind. These advances are real, but an honest appraisal will show, I think, that they are far from providing such a key. We do not understand, and for all we know, we may never come to understand what makes it possible for a normal human intelligence to use language as an instrument for the free expression of thought and feeling; or, for that matter, what qualities of mind are involved in the creative acts of intelligence that are characteristic, not unique and exceptional, in a truly human existence.

I think that this is an important fact to stress, not only for linguists and psychologists whose research centers on these issues, but, even more, for those who hope to learn something useful in their own work and thinking from research into language and thought. It is particularly important that the limitations of understanding be clear to those involved in teaching, in the universities, and even more important, in the schools. There are strong pressures to make use of new educational technology and to design curriculum and teaching methods in the light of the latest scientific advances. In itself, this is not objectionable. It is important, nevertheless, to remain alert to a very real danger: that new knowledge and technique will define the nature of what is taught and how it is taught, rather than contribute to the realization of educational goals that are set on other grounds and in other terms. Let me be concrete. Technique and even technology is available for rapid and efficient inculcation of skilled behavior, in language teaching, teaching of arithmetic, and other domains. There is, consequently, a real temptation to reconstruct curriculum in the terms defined by the new technology. And it is not too difficult to invent a rationale, making use of the concepts of "controlling behavior," enhancing skills, and so on. Nor is it difficult to construct objective tests that are sure to demonstrate the effectiveness of such methods in reaching certain goals that are incorporated in these tests. But successes of this sort will not demonstrate that an important educational goal has been achieved. They will not demonstrate that it is important to concentrate on developing skilled behavior in the student. What little we know about human intelligence would at least suggest something quite different: that by diminishing the range and complexity of materials presented to the inquiring mind, by setting behavior in fixed patterns, these methods may harm and distort the normal development of creative abilities. I do not want to dwell on the matter. I am sure that any of you will be able to find examples from your own experience. It is perfectly proper to try to exploit genuine advances in knowledge, and within some given field of study, it is inevitable, and quite proper, that research should be directed by considerations of feasibility as well as considerations of ultimate significance. It is also highly likely, if not inevitable, that considerations of feasibility and significance will lead in divergent paths. For those who wish to apply the achievements of one discipline to the problems of another, it is important to make very clear the exact nature not only of what has been achieved, but equally important, the limitations of what has been achieved.

I mentioned a moment ago that the creative aspect of normal use of language is not a new discovery. It provides one important pillar for Descartes' theory of mind, for his study of the limits of mechanical explanation. The latter, in turn, provides one crucial element in the construction of the anti-authoritarian social and political philosophy of the Enlightenment. And, in fact, there were even some efforts to found a theory of artistic creativity on the creative aspect of normal language use. Schlegel, for example, argues that poetry has a unique position among the arts, a fact illustrated, he claims, by the use of the term poetical" to refer to the element of creative imagination in any artistic effort, as distinct, say, from the term "musical," which would be used metaphorically to refer to a sensual element. To explain this asymmetry, he observes that every mode of artistic expression makes use of a certain medium and that the medium of poetry -- language -- is unique in that language, as an expression of the human mind rather than a product of nature, is boundless in scope and is constructed on the basis of a recursive principle that permits each creation to serve as the basis for a new creative act. Hence the central position among the arts of the art forms whose medium is language.

The belief that language, with its inherent creative aspect, is a unique human possession did not go unchallenged, of course. One expositor of Cartesian philosophy, Antoine Le Grand, refers to the opinion "of some people of the East Indies, who think that Apes and Baboons, which are with them in great numbers, are imbued with understanding, and that they can speak but will not for fear they should be employed, and set to work." If there is a more serious argument in support of the claim that human language capacity is shared with other primates, then I am unaware of it. In fact, whatever evidence we do have seems to me to support the view that the ability to acquire and use language is a species-specific human capacity, that there are very deep and restrictive principles that determine the nature of human language and are rooted in the specific character of the human mind. Obviously arguments bearing on this hypothesis cannot be definitive or conclusive, but it appears to me, nevertheless, that even in the present stage of our knowledge, the evidence is not inconsiderable.

There are any number of questions that might lead one to undertake a study of language. Personally, I am primarily intrigued by the possibility of learning something, from the study of language, that will bring to light inherent properties of the human mind. We cannot now say anything particularly informative about the normal creative use of language in itself. But I think that we are slowly coming to understand the mechanisms that make possible this creative use of language, the use of language as an instrument of free thought and expression. Speaking again from a personal point of view, to me the most interesting aspects of contemporary work in grammar are the attempts to formulate principles of organization of language which, it is proposed, are universal reflections of properties of mind; and the attempt to show that on this assumption, certain facts about particular languages can be explained. Viewed in this way, linguistics is simply a part of human psychology: the field that seeks to determine the nature of human mental capacities and to study how these capacities are put to work. Many psychologists would reject a characterization of their discipline in these terms, but this reaction seems to me to indicate a serious inadequacy in their conception of psychology, rather than a defect in the formulation itself. In any event, it seems to me that these are proper terms in which to set the goals of contemporary linguistics, and to discuss its achievements and its failings.

I think it is now possible to make some fairly definite proposals about the organization of human language and to put them to empirical test. The theory of transformational-generative grammar, as it is evolving along diverse and sometimes conflicting paths, has put forth such proposals; and there has been, in the past few years, some very productive and suggestive work that attempts to refine and reconstruct these formulations of the processes and structures that underlie human language.

The theory of grammar is concerned with the question, What is the nature of a person's knowledge of his language, the knowledge that enables him to make use of language in the normal, creative fashion? A person who knows a language has mastered a system of rules that assigns sound and meaning in a definite way for an infinite class of possible sentences. Each language thus consists (in part) of a certain pairing of sound and meaning over an infinite domain. Of course, the person who knows the language has no consciousness of having mastered these rules or of putting them to use, nor is there any reason to suppose that this knowledge of the rules of language can be brought to consciousness. Through introspection, a person may accumulate various kinds of evidence about the sound-meaning relation determined by the rules of the language that he has mastered; there is no reason to suppose that he can go much beyond this surface level of data so as to discover, through introspection, the underlying rules and principles that determine the relation of sound and meaning. Rather, to discover these rules and principles is a typical problem of science. We have a collection of data regarding sound-meaning correspondence, the form and interpretation of linguistic expressions, in various languages. We try to determine, for each language, a system of rules that will account for such data. More deeply, we try to establish the principles that govern the formation of such systems of rules for any human language.

The system of rules that specifies the sound-meaning relation for a given language can be called the "grammar" -- or, to use a more technical term, the "generative grammar" of this language. To say that a grammar "generates" a certain set of structures is simply to say that it specifies this set in a precise way. In this sense, we may say that the grammar of a language generates an infinite set of "structural descriptions," each structural description being an abstract object of some sort that determines a particular sound, a particular meaning, and whatever formal properties and configurations serve to mediate the relation between sound and meaning. For example, the grammar of English generates structural descriptions for the sentences I am now speaking; or, to take a simpler case for purposes of illustration, the grammar of English would generate a structural description for each of these sentences:

1. **John is certain that Bill will leave.**
2. **John is certain to leave.**

Each of us has mastered and internally represented a system of grammar that assigns structural descriptions to these sentences; we use this knowledge, totally without awareness or even the possibility of awareness, in producing these sentences or understanding them when they are produced by others. The structural descriptions include a phonetic representation of the sentences and a specification of their meaning. In the case of the cited examples 1 and 2, the structural descriptions must convey roughly the following information: They must indicate that in the case of 1, a given psychological state (namely, being certain that Bill will leave) is attributed to John; whereas in the case of 2, a given logical property (namely, the property of being certain) is attributed to the proposition that John will leave. Despite the superficial similarity of form of these two sentences, the structural descriptions generated by the grammar must indicate that their meanings are very different: One attributes a psychological state to John, the other attributes a logical property to an abstract proposition. The second sentence might be paraphrased in a very different form:

3. **That John will leave is certain.**

For the first there is no such paraphrase. In the paraphrase 3 the "logical form" of 2 is expressed more directly, one might say. The grammatical relations in 2 and 3 are very similar, despite the difference of surface form; the grammatical relations in 1 and 2 are very different, despite the similarity of surface form. Such facts as these provide the starting point for an investigation of the grammatical structure of English -- and more generally, for the investigation of the general properties of human language.

To carry the discussion of properties of language further, let me introduce the term "surface structure" to refer to a representation of the phrases that constitute a linguistic expression and the categories to which these phrases belong. In sentence 1, the phrases of the surface structure include: "that Bill will leave," which is a full proposition; the noun phrases "Bill" and "John"; the verb phrases "will leave" and "is certain that Bill will leave," and so on. In sentence 2, the surface structure includes the verb phrases "to leave" and "is certain to leave"; but the surface structure of 2 includes no proposition of the form "John will leave," even though this proposition expresses part of the meaning of "John is certain to leave," and appears as a phrase in the surface structure of its paraphrase, "that John will leave is certain." In this sense, surface structure does not necessarily provide an accurate indication of the structures and relations that determine the meaning of a sentence; in the case of sentence 2, "John is certain to leave," the surface structure fails to indicate that the proposition "John will leave" expresses a part of the meaning of the sentence -- although in the other two examples that I gave the surface structure comes rather close to indicating the semantically significant relations.

Continuing, let me introduce the further technical term "deep structure" to refer to a representation of the phrases that play a more central role in the semantic interpretation of a sentence. In the case of 1 and 3, the deep structure might not be very different from the surface structure. In the case of 2, the deep structure will be very different from the surface structure, in that it will include some such proposition as "John will leave" and the predicate "is certain" applied to this proposition, though nothing of the sort appears in the surface structure. In general, apart from the simplest examples, the surface structures of sentences are very different from their deep structures.

The grammar of English will generate, for each sentence, a deep structure, and will contain rules showing how this deep structure is related to a surface structure. The rules expressing the relation of deep and surface structure are called "grammatical transformations." Hence the term "transformational-generative grammar." In addition to rules defining deep structures, surface structures, and the relation between them, the grammar of English contains further rules that relate these "syntactic objects" (namely, paired deep and surface structures) to phonetic representations on the one hand, and to representations of meaning on the other. A person who has acquired knowledge of English has internalized these rules and makes use of them when he understands or produces the sentences just given as examples, and an indefinite range of others.

Evidence in support of this approach is provided by the observation that interesting properties of English sentences can be explained directly in terms of the deep structures assigned to them. Thus consider once again the two sentences 1 ("John is certain that Bill will leave") and 2 ("John is certain to leave"). Recall that in the case of the first, the deep structure and surface structure are virtually identical, whereas in the case of the second, they are very different. Observe also that in the case of the first, there is a corresponding nominal phrase, namely, "John's certainty that Bill will leave (surprised me)"; but in the case of the second, there is no corresponding nominal phrase. We cannot say "John's certainty to leave surprised me." The latter nominal phrase is intelligible, 1 suppose, but it is not well formed in English. The speaker of English can easily make himself aware of this fact, though the reason for it will very likely escape him. This fact is a special case of a very general property of English: Namely, nominal phrases exist corresponding to sentences that are very close in surface form to deep structure, but not corresponding to such sentences that are remote in surface form from deep structure. Thus "John is certain that Bill will leave," being close in surface form to its deep structure, corresponds to the nominal phrase "John's certainty that Bill will leave"; but there is no such phrase as "John's certainty to leave" corresponding to "John is certain to leave," which is remote from its deep structure.

The notions of "closeness" and "remoteness" can be made quite precise. When we have made them precise, we have an explanation for the fact that nominalizations exist in certain cases but not in others -- though were they to exist in these other cases, they would often be perfectly intelligible. The explanation turns on the notion of deep structure: In effect, it states that nominalizations must reflect the properties of deep structure. There are many examples that illustrate this phenomenon. What is important is the evidence it provides in support of the view that deep structures which are often quite abstract exist and play a central role in the grammatical processes that we use in producing and interpreting sentences. Such facts, then, support the hypothesis that deep structures of the sort postulated in transformational-generative grammar are real mental structures. These deep structures, along with the transformation rules that relate them to surface structure and the rules relating deep and surface structures to representations of sound and meaning, are the rules that have been mastered by the person who has learned a language. They constitute his knowledge of the language; they are put to use when he speaks and understands.

The examples I have given so far illustrate the role of deep structure in determining meaning, and show that even in very simple cases, the deep structure may be remote from the surface form. There is a great deal of evidence indicating that the phonetic form of a sentence is determined by its surface structure, by principles of an extremely interesting and intricate sort that I will not try to discuss here. From such evidence it is fair to conclude that surface structure determines phonetic form, and that the grammatical relations represented in deep structure are those that determine meaning. Furthermore, as already noted, there are certain grammatical processes, such as the process of nominalization, that can be stated only in terms of abstract deep structures.

The situation is complicated, however, by the fact that surface structure also plays a role in determining semantic interpretation.[1] The study of this question is one of the most controversial aspects of current work, and, in my opinion, likely to be one of the most fruitful. As an illustration, consider some of the properties of the present perfect aspect in English -- for example, such sentences as "John has lived in Princeton." An interesting and rarely noted feature of this aspect is that in such cases it carries the presupposition that the subject is alive. Thus it is proper for me to say "I have lived in Princeton" but, knowing that Einstein is dead, I would not say "Einstein has lived in Princeton." Rather, I would say "Einstein lived in Princeton." (As always, there are complications, but this is accurate as a first approximation.) But now consider active and passive forms with present perfect aspect. Knowing that John is dead and Bill alive, I can say "Bill has often been visited by John," but not "John has often visited Bill"; rather, "John often visited Bill." I can say "I have been taught physics by Einstein" but not "Einstein has taught me physics"; rather, "Einstein taught me physics." In general, active and passive are synonymous and have

---

[1] I discuss this matter in some detail in "Deep Structure and Semantic Interpretation," in R. Jakobson, and S. Kawamoto, eds., *Studies in General and Oriental Linguistics*, commemorative volume for Shiro Hattori, TEC Corporation for Language and Educational Research, Tokyo, 1970.

essentially the same deep structures. But in these cases, active and passive forms differ in the presuppositions they express; put simply, the presupposition is that the person denoted by the surface subject is alive. In this respect, the surface structure contributes to the meaning of the sentence in that it is relevant to determining what is presupposed in the use of a sentence.

Carrying the matter further, observe that the situation is different when we have a conjoined subject. Thus given that Hilary is alive and Marco Polo dead, it is proper to say "Hilary has climbed Mt. Everest" but not "Marco Polo has climbed Mt. Everest"; rather, again, "Marco Polo climbed Mt. Everest." (Again, I overlook certain subtleties and complications.) But now consider the sentence "Marco Polo and Hilary (among others) have climbed Mt. Everest." In this case, there is no expressed presupposition that Marco Polo is alive, as there is none in the passive "Mt. Everest has been climbed by Marco Polo (among others)."

Notice further that the situation changes considerably when we shift from the normal intonation, as in the cases I have just given, to an intonation contour that contains a contrastive or expressive stress. The effect of such intonation on presupposition is fairly complex. Let me illustrate with a simple case. Consider the sentence "The Yankees played the Red Sox in Boston." With normal intonation, the point of main stress and highest pitch is the word "Boston" and the sentence might be an answer to such questions as "where did the Yankees play the Red Sox?" ("in Boston"); "what did the Yankees do?" ("they played the Red Sox in Boston"); "what happened?" ("the Yankees played the Red Sox in Boston"). But suppose that contrastive stress is placed on "Red Sox so that we have "The Yankees played the Red Sox in Boston." Now, the sentence can be the answer only to "Who did the Yankees play in Boston?" Note that the sentence presupposes that the Yankees played someone in Boston; if there was no game at all, it is improper, not just false, to say "The Yankees played the Red Sox in Boston." In contrast, if there was no game at all, it is false, but not improper, to say The Yankees played the Red Sox in Boston," with normal intonation. Thus contrastive stress carries a presupposition in a sense in which normal intonation does not, though normal intonation also carries a presupposition in another sense; thus it would be improper to answer the question "Who played the Red Sox in Boston?" with "The Yankees played the Red Sox in Boston" (normal intonation). The same property of contrastive stress is shown by the so-called cleft sentence construction. Thus the sentence "It was the YANKEES who played the Red Sox in Boston" has primary stress on "Yankees," and presupposes that someone played the Red Sox in Boston. The sentence is improper, not just false, if there was no game at all. These phenomena have generally been overlooked when the semantic role of contrastive stress has been noted.

To further illustrate the role of surface structure in determining meaning, consider such sentences as this: "John is tall for a pygmy. This sentence presupposes that John is a pygmy, and that pygmies tend to be short; hence given our knowledge of the Watusi, it would be anomalous to say "John is tall for a Watusi." On the other hand, consider what happens when we insert the word "even" in the sentence. Inserting it before "John" we derive: "Even John is tall for a pygmy. Again, the presupposition is that John is a pygmy and that pygmies are short. But consider: "John is tall even for a pygmy." This presupposes that pygmies are tall; it is therefore a strange sentence, given our knowledge of the facts, as compared, say, to "John is tall even for a Watusi," which is quite all right. The point is that the position of "even" in the sentence "John is tall for a pygmy" determines the presupposition with respect to the average height of pygmies.

But the placement of the word "even" is a matter of surface structure. We can see this from the fact that the word "even" can appear in association with phrases that do not have any representation at the level of deep structure: Consider, for example, the sentence "John isn't certain to leave at 10; in fact, he isn't even certain to leave at all." Here, the word "even" is associated with "certain to leave," a phrase which, as noted earlier, does not appear at the level of deep structure. Hence in this case as well properties of surface structure play a role in determining what is presupposed by a certain sentence.

The role of surface structure in determining meaning is illustrated once again by the phenomenon of pronominalization.[2] Thus if I say "Each of the men hates his brothers," the word "his" may refer to one of the men; but if I say "The men each hate his brothers," the word "his" must refer to some other person, not otherwise referred to in the sentence. However, the evidence is strong that "each of the men" and "the men each" derive from the same deep structure. Similarly, it has been noted that placement of stress plays an important role in determining pronominal reference. Consider the following discourse: "John washed the car; I was afraid someone ELSE would do it." The sentence implies that I hoped that John would wash the car, and I'm happy that he did. But now consider the following: "John washed the car; I was AFRAID someone else would do it." With stress on "afraid," the sentence implies that I hoped that John would not wash the car. The reference of "someone else" is different in the two cases. There are many other examples that illustrate the role of surface structure in determining pronominal reference.

To complicate matters still further, deep structure too plays a role in determining pronominal reference. Thus consider the sentence "John appeared to Bill to like him." Here, the pronoun "him" may refer to Bill but not John. Compare "John appealed to Bill to like him." Here, the pronoun may refer to John but not Bill. Thus we can say "John appealed to Mary to like him," but not "John appeared to Mary to like him," where "him" refers to "John"; on the other hand,

---

[2] The examples that follow are due to Ray Dougherty, Adrian Akmajian, and Ray Jackendoff. See my article in Jakobson and Kawamoto, eds., *Studies in General and Oriental Linguistics*, for references

we can say "John appeared to Mary to like her," but not "John appealed to Mary to like her," where "her" refers to Mary. Similarly, in "John appealed to Bill to like himself," the reflexive refers to Bill; but in "John appeared to Bill to like himself," it refers to John. These sentences are approximately the same in surface structure; it is the differences in deep structure that determine the pronominal reference.

Hence pronominal reference depends on both deep and surface structure. A person who knows English has mastered a system of rules which make use of properties of deep and surface structure in determining pronominal reference. Again, he cannot discover these rules by introspection. In fact, these rules are still unknown, though some of their properties are clear.

To summarize: The generative grammar of a language specifies an infinite set of structural descriptions, each of which contains a deep structure, a surface structure, a phonetic representation, a semantic representation, and other formal structures. The rules relating deep and surface structure -- the so-called "grammatical transformations" -- have been investigated in some detail, and are fairly well understood. The rules that relate surface structure and phonetic representation are also reasonably well understood (though I do not want to imply that the matter is beyond dispute; far from it). It seems that both deep and surface structure enter into the determination of meaning. Deep structure provides the grammatical relations of predication, modification, and so on, that enter into the determination of meaning. On the other hand, it appears that matters of focus and presupposition, topic and comment, the scope of logical elements, and pronominal reference are determined, in part at least, by surface structure. The rules that relate syntactic structures to representations of meaning are not at all well understood. In fact, the notion "representation of meaning or semantic representation" is itself highly controversial. It is not clear at all that it is possible to distinguish sharply between the contribution of grammar to the determination of meaning, and the contribution of so-called "pragmatic considerations," questions of fact and belief and context of utterance. It is perhaps worth mentioning that rather similar questions can be raised about the notion "phonetic representation." Although the latter is one of the best established and least controversial notions of linguistic theory, we can; nevertheless, raise the question whether or not it is a legitimate abstraction, whether a deeper understanding of the use of language might not show that factors that go beyond grammatical structure enter into the determination of perceptual representations and physical form in an inextricable fashion, and cannot be separated, without distortion, from the formal rules that interpret surface structure as phonetic form.

So far, the study of language has progressed on the basis of a certain abstraction: Namely, we abstract away from conditions of use of language and consider formal structures and the formal operations that relate them. Among these formal structures are those of syntax, namely, deep and surface structures; and also the phonetic and semantic representations, which we take to be certain formal objects related to syntactic structures by certain well-defined operations. This process of abstraction is in no way illegitimate, but one must understand that it expresses a point of view, a hypothesis about the nature of mind, that is not a priori obvious. It expresses the working hypothesis that we can proceed with the study of "knowledge of language" -- what is often called "linguistic competence" -- in abstraction from the problems of how language is used. The working hypothesis is justified by the success that is achieved when it is adopted. A great deal has been learned about the mechanisms of language, and, I would say, about the nature of mind, on the basis of this hypothesis. But we must be aware that in part, at least, this approach to language is forced upon us by the fact that our concepts fail us when we try to study the use of language. We are reduced to platitudes, or to observations which, though perhaps quite interesting, do not lend themselves to systematic study by means of the intellectual tools presently available to us. On the other hand, we can bring to the study of formal structures and their relations a wealth of experience and understanding. It may be that at this point we are facing a problem of conflict between significance and feasibility, a conflict of the sort that I mentioned earlier in this paper. I do not believe that this is the case, but it is possible. I feel fairly confident that the abstraction to the study of formal mechanisms of language is appropriate; my confidence arises from the fact that many quite elegant results have been achieved on the basis of this abstraction. Still, caution is in order. It may be that the next great advance in the study of language will require the forging of new intellectual tools that permit us to bring into consideration a variety of questions that have been cast into the waste-bin of "pragmatics," so that we could proceed to study questions that we know how to formulate in an intelligible fashion.

As noted, I think that the abstraction to linguistic competence is legitimate. To go further, I believe that the inability of modern psychology to come to grips with the problems of human intelligence is in part, at least, a result of its unwillingness to undertake the study of abstract structures and mechanisms of mind. Notice that the approach to linguistic structure that I have been outlining has a highly traditional flavor to it. I think it is no distortion to say that this approach makes precise a point of view that was inherent in the very important work of the seventeenth- and eighteenth-century universal grammarians, and that was developed, in various ways, in rationalist and romantic philosophy of language and mind. The approach deviates in many ways from a more modern, and in my opinion quite erroneous conception that knowledge of language can be accounted for as a system of habits, or in terms of stimulus-response connections, principles of "analogy" and "generalization," and other notions that have been explored in twentieth-century linguistics and psychology, and that develop from traditional empiricist speculation. The fatal inadequacy of all such approaches, I believe, results from their unwillingness to undertake the abstract study of linguistic competence. Had the physical sciences limited themselves by similar methodological strictures, we would still be in the era of Babylonian astronomy.

One traditional concept that has reemerged in current work is that of "universal grammar," and I want to conclude by saying just a word about this topic. There are two kinds of evidence suggesting that deepseated formal conditions are satisfied by the grammars of all languages. The first kind of evidence is provided by the study of a wide range of languages. In attempting to construct generative grammars for languages of widely varied kinds, investigators have repeatedly been led to rather similar assumptions as to the form and organization of such generative systems. But a more persuasive kind of evidence bearing on universal grammar is provided by the study of a single language. It may at first seem paradoxical that the intensive study of a single language should provide evidence regarding universal grammar, but a little thought about the matter shows that this is a very natural consequence.

To see this, consider the problem of determining the mental capacities that make language acquisition possible. If the study of grammar -- of linguistic competence -- involves an abstraction from language use, then the study of the mental capacities that make acquisition of grammar possible involves a further, second-order abstraction. I see no fault in this. We may formulate the problem of determining the intrinsic characteristics of a device of unknown properties that accepts as "input" the kind of data available to the child learning his first language, and produces as "output" the generative grammar of that language. The "output," in this case, is the internally represented grammar, mastery of which constitutes knowledge of the language. If we undertake to study the intrinsic structure of a language-acquisition device without dogma or prejudice, we arrive at conclusions which, though of course only tentative, still seem to me both significant and reasonably well-founded. We must attribute to this device enough structure so that the grammar can be constructed within the empirically given constraints of time and available data, and we must meet the empirical condition that different speakers of the same language, with somewhat different experience and training, nevertheless acquire grammars that are remarkably similar, as we can determine from the ease with which they communicate and the correspondences among them in the interpretation of new sentences. It is immediately obvious that the data available to the child is quite limited -- the number of seconds in his lifetime is trivially small as compared with the range of sentences that he can immediately understand and can produce in the appropriate manner. Having some knowledge of the characteristics of the acquired grammars and the limitations on the available data, we can formulate quite reasonable and fairly strong empirical hypotheses regarding the internal structure of the language-acquisition device that constructs the postulated grammars from the given data. When we study this question in detail, we are, I believe, led to attribute to the device a very rich system of constraints on the form of a possible grammar; otherwise, it is impossible to explain how children come to construct grammars of the kind that seem empirically adequate under the given conditions of time and access to data. But if we assume, furthermore, that children are not genetically predisposed to learn one rather than another language, then the conclusions we reach regarding the language-acquisition device are conclusions regarding universal grammar. These conclusions can be falsified by showing that they fail to account for the construction of grammars of other languages, for example. And these conclusions are further verified if they serve to explain facts about other languages. This line of argument seems to me very reasonable in a general way, and when pursued in detail it leads us to strong empirical hypotheses concerning universal grammar, even from the study of a particular language.

I have discussed an approach to the study of language that takes this study to be a branch of theoretical human psychology. Its goal is to exhibit and clarify the mental capacities that make it possible for a human to learn and use a language. As far as we know, these capacities are unique to man, and have no significant analogue in any other organism. If the conclusions of this research are anywhere near correct, then humans must be endowed with a very rich and explicit set of mental attributes that determine a specific form of language on the basis of very slight and rather degenerate data. Furthermore, they make use of the mentally represented language in a highly creative way, constrained by its rules but free to express new thoughts that relate to past experience or present sensations only in a remote and abstract fashion. If this is correct, there is no hope in the study of the "control" of human behavior by stimulus conditions, schedules of reinforcement, establishment of habit structures, patterns of behavior, and so on. Of course, one can design a restricted environment in which such control and such patterns can be demonstrated, but there is no reason to suppose that any more is learned about the range of human potentialities by such methods than would be learned by observing humans in a prison or an army -- or in many a schoolroom. The essential properties of the human mind will always escape such investigation. And if I can be pardoned a final "non-professional" comment, I am very happy with this outcome.